Luke 1:37

AMEN AND BEYOND

For With God Nothing Is ever
Impossible And No Word from
God shall be Without Power
or Impossible of fulfillment.

The Amplified Bible

R O N   M I K E L S

AMEN AND BEYOND

HEALING PRAYER STRATEGIES
THAT CAN CHANGE YOUR LIFE

Unless otherwise noted, all Scriptures are taken from the King James Version of the Holy Scriptures.

Scripture references marked HCSB are taken from the Holman Christian Standard Bible®. Copyright ©1999, 2000, 2002, 2003 by Holman Bible Publishers. Used by permission. Holman Christian Standard Bible®, Holman CSB®, and HCSB® are federally registered trademarks of Holman Bible Publishers.

Scripture references marked AMP are taken from The Amplified Bible, Old Testament copyright © 1965, 1987 by the Zondervan Corporation. The Amplified New Testament copyright ©1958, 1987 by The Lockman Foundation. Used by permission.

Lovingly dedicated to
the Great Physician,
and to
Norma, my beloved wife,
without whom this book could not have been
written,
and to our special son Rick and his Meghan

TABLE OF CONTENTS

PREFACE

Prayer is our primary means of communication with God so it is imperative that we become familiar with the principles of speaking with our heavenly Father.

When Christ walked on the earth, He provided everything His followers needed with respect to food, money, and healing. When He ascended to heaven, He told His disciples to pray and "whatsoever ye shall ask the Father in my name, he will give it you" (John 16:23).

There are various methods we can employ to enhance our times of communion with God.

This book deals primarily with prayers of asking for and receiving healing from God. There are other types of prayer that we do not deal with here:

the prayer of dedication and worship, intercessory prayer, and the prayer of binding and loosing. Perhaps we can explore these in another volume.

I am well aware that the prayer accounts herein may seem extreme or "far out" to some. But we are on solid spiritual ground as long as they agree with the written Word.

A short while back, I was rather smug about my own prayer beliefs, even avoiding asking others to help us pray when the need arose. Then my wife was stricken with a very painful ruptured disk. At that point, I welcomed any and all prayers from others. I was humbled and remain so.

It is my hope that you may adapt one or more of these prayer strategies to your own situation and reap similar results. These principles have literally changed my life. They can change yours as well!

Special Notes: If you are ill, you should be under the care of a doctor or other healthcare provider. Do not change your medications without his or her approval. As the healing power of Christ begins to work in your body, you may then ask your doctor to alter your medications.

Some names have been changed to protect the individual's privacy.

INTRODUCTION

A hush came over the congregation as the organist rendered "A Mighty Fortress Is Our God." The smiling choir marched in, adorned in their new royal blue robes.

Everyone was waiting to get the first glimpse of our new pastor on his first Sunday at Dandridge Avenue Methodist. Young, tall and distinguished looking, Rev. W seemed to be just what we needed. I hoped he would be involved in my youth group.

Hearing a few whispers during the pastoral prayer, I thought it was just the result of "new pastor jitters." But within five minutes of returning home that day, a church member telephoned my mom and asked, "Did you notice that the new preacher only knelt on *one* knee during his prayer? Rev. F always knelt on both knees. Do you suppose he's really a Christian?"

But Rev. W continued to pray on one knee and went on to become one of our most illustrious and evangelical pastors, leading us through a period of rapid growth and a successful building campaign.

I knew almost nothing about prayer in those early years, except I felt it was something only pastors were supposed to do. Had I been more experienced in prayer, I reasoned later, I might have prevented the untimely death of my dad when I was in the eleventh grade.

The school administrator summoned me to the high school office that day and sent me home immediately. A family friend was waiting to rush me to the hospital, but even the best medical care of the day couldn't save my dad from a massive coronary. Had I somehow failed him? Were my feeble prayers not enough? I began a learning experience that continues to this day.

I had no clue as to the exciting part prayer would play in my life, especially in my search for a wife.

CHAPTER 1

HEAVENLY SUNLIGHT

Everyone move to the back of the room. We're having an orientation up here in just a few minutes," announced our teacher, Mr. White.

About twenty new summer students marched into the front of the third floor accounting room at Knoxville Business College. Among them was one of the prettiest young ladies I had ever seen. I'll call her Evelyn. I made it a point to introduce myself at the beginning of the next class, and I accompanied her to the bus stop every day after school. Within just a few weeks, I fell in love with this Christian young lady who was intelligent enough to converse on almost any subject.

But it wasn't to last. After dating several months, she met me at the school's front entrance early one Monday morning. "Ronald, I need to talk to you." She had begun dating someone else and asked me not to call her again. Crushed, I tried to get on with my studies. But the hurt was real and seemingly permanent.

It was worse during Christmas. As I roamed a shopping mall one evening, I noticed a young man and his girlfriend window shopping for an engagement ring. The loneliness of the past few years gnawed at me. Silently I prayed, "Father, please send me someone. I don't care who—just as long as she's pretty."

I had no idea that God had already set in motion the factors that would bring me together with the person He had chosen for me. Norma's boss, a vice president at the bank where we both worked, had introduced us a few months earlier. I wondered then if she was married. I asked a co-worker and discovered she was single. Plus, she had the most captivating blue eyes I'd ever seen. Could she be the girl I'd been searching for? I learned later she had the same questions about me.

After dating for only a short while, we announced our engagement and planned to marry. We believed that we had been brought together by the Lord. But both of us had second thoughts since we had been serious about others before we met. Was this the right step? Hoping for the best, we decided to press on with our plans.

"Are you ready to elope with me?" I telephoned my bride-to-be at 5:00 a.m.

She managed a sleepy "Yes," and we were soon on the way to see our former minister in Chattanooga. Opting for a quiet wedding, we drove a hundred snowy miles in bone-chilling weather and married in the new church's temporary sanctuary.

While exchanging vows, it seemed as if God Himself were watching as a soft glow enveloped us. Or was it just my imagination? I didn't mention it, thinking no one else had noticed.

The years rushed by while we raised our son and worked demanding jobs. I almost forgot the incident. We hadn't been inside the church again until now, three decades later.

The elegant structure was nearly full for the morning service. After the last "Amen," we asked an usher to show us the old sanctuary. He graciously led us down a long hallway and into the musty room. I recognized it at once.

"Norma, we stood just about here," I remarked as we entered, pointing to a spot near the door.

"No, Ron, it had to be on the far side of the room, under the windows. There are no windows over here." She seemed certain of the location. And

I was equally sure the spot was near the door, but said nothing until we returned to the car.

"Why do you think we were married on the other side?" I asked.

"Because there must have been windows above us that day. I distinctly remember the sun came from behind the clouds and started shining on us during the ceremony. I thought it was God's way of approving our marriage," she said.

I recalled my own experience and shared it with her for the first time. She stared at me in amazement. "Ron, you saw the same thing? Then there weren't any windows?"

Yes, we had chosen the right course that winter day so many years ago.

We headed home in the brilliant sunlight.

CHAPTER 2

WHEN GOD IS SILENT

All of us have encountered situations when our prayers seem to go unanswered, even when we enlist the help of scores of prayer warriors who fast and intercede for us. Why is God silent? Are there prayer guidelines that ensure that we have the ear of God? Here is a partial list:

- *The only prayer that God hears from sinners is the prayer of repentance.* Therefore, if you are a sinner, you are spinning your wheels with any other prayer. Read over the prayer below. If you honestly believe the words and can pray it with sincerity, do so now:

Dear Heavenly Father, I come to you in the name of Jesus to obtain forgiveness for my sins and to inherit eternal life. I truly believe that Jesus Christ is Your Son, and that He died for my sins. I believe that You raised Him from the dead and that He ascended back into heaven. I now receive Jesus Christ into my heart and claim Him as my Savior. Please come into my heart and cleanse me of all sins. Thank You, Lord!

If you sincerely prayed this prayer, you are now a child of God. You have just experienced a miracle greater than physical healing. Praise His Name!

- Suppose you are praying for someone who is ill and you have not seen the results of your prayers. *In these cases, we must always consider the wishes of the one who is ill.*

Take the case of a young man in his late teens who was attending Bible college. Hearing that his uncle was ill, he submitted prayer requests regularly at their daily assemblies. He fasted, prayed, and believed with all his heart, standing on several Scriptures.

But his uncle died. After returning from the funeral, he asked the head of the college why his uncle hadn't been healed. The wise administrator simply asked him, "What did your uncle want? Did he really want to be healed?"

"No, he wanted to go on to heaven."

That's self-explanatory. Ordinarily, we can't override the personal wishes of others in prayer. And we can never be certain of their standing with the Lord.

Even though God sometimes answers our prayers differently than we expect, He always answers according to His Word.

• *We must also remember that God's clock many times runs more slowly than we like.* I recall the time that I had to wait for four years and five months for an answer to a personal prayer.

My family was in Nashville, Tennessee, on Thanksgiving Day in 1987. We attended services sponsored by Rhema Bible College and its founder, Rev. Kenneth E. Hagin. At the end of the service, Brother Hagin announced, "I've only done this once or twice in my ministry, but I want everyone who has anything wrong with them from the hips down to come forward for prayer. We have several ministers here who will pray for you."

I had suffered severe back pains for nineteen years as the result of a fall on an icy pavement. A motion as slight as bending over to rinse my razor in the sink would cause me to scream out in pain.

Some years later, I discovered that my hamstrings were extremely tight. After exercises to loosen them, some of the discomfort left but the basic pain was still there.

I consulted several orthopedic surgeons and chiropractors. I even flew to New Orleans to consult with an osteopathic physician. They were able to give some temporary relief, but because I had a congenitally short left leg, the pain always returned within hours of being treated.

So I went forward, and one of the ministers prayed that my left leg would be lengthened one-quarter inch to make it even with the right. I felt nothing at the time, but the minister assured me that he felt the power of God go into my legs and that I should just continue to believe. I promised him that I would.

One evening several years later, I was lying across the bed reading the newspaper. Suddenly, waves of electricity came upon my left upper leg, lasting for several seconds. Since it had been so long since the prayer, I didn't immediately connect the two. But I knew it was of God and said, "Thank You, Lord."

Then I began experiencing pain in my right hip. I found it difficult to get out of my car and I could barely walk from the elevator to my office. I had to find a parking place closer to the office because of the pain.

After several days of intense pain, I wondered. Could it be? Having seen two orthopedic doctors, three chiropractors, and an osteopathic physician for pain in the past, I remembered how to measure the length of my legs. When I measured, I discovered that, for the first time since birth, my legs measured the same.

I took my shoes to the shoe shop for correction the next morning. I had been wearing a built-up heel and sole for twenty-three years. After the elevations were removed, I had no further trouble.

Yes, God moved more slowly that I had hoped, but I was just as happy almost four and a half years later as I would have been had the miracle been manifest that same night in 1987.

When God doesn't answer immediately, some intelligent, God-fearing Christians believe that He may be trying to teach us a lesson. That's a possibility and even a necessity if we don't follow God's leading. But in reviewing the gospel accounts of Jesus' healing ministry, He never refused to heal, saying, "No, God is trying to teach you something."

Instead, we read that He healed them all (Matthew 8:16-17, 12:15, Luke 4:40).

Try to imagine this scenario: You have been lax in your tithing for the past two years. So God says, "Let's give him cancer to teach him to give more often." No, a loving Father would never put a disease on His child.

God chastises us in love, but it is not always comfortable. If we don't respond, it could become more serious.

We must live a holy life, totally committed to God (Leviticus 11:44). *Holy* and *holiness* are mentioned more than six hundred times in the Bible. And we must listen for the voice of God. His Holy Spirit will guide us. If we stray, we could leave ourselves open to an attack from the enemy which is often incorrectly blamed on God.

- *At times, I believe God protects us by restraining our impatience.* When I was about 37 years old, I worked as EDP Auditor for a large regional bank. On Christmas Eve, we wanted to speed up our usual 24-hour computer processing so our night shift could get home in time for Christmas.

We contacted all our offices and asked them to have their checks and deposits ready early and told them that we would personally pick them up, rather than leave them for the armored trucks. One of the programmers and I were to pick up in the northern area of the city. When we arrived at one of our branches, there was a delay because the work was not yet microfilmed. We waited . . . and waited, fuming all the while. Little did we know the fate we may have encountered had we left on time.

When we finally received the items, we drove southward on Highway 33 toward the computer center. Within a couple of blocks, we came upon the aftermath of a deadly automobile crash involving three mangled vehicles. Bodies were lying on the highway; good Samaritans, trying to help, were fainting and falling over. It seems that a driver, apparently drinking heavily, had backed out of a tavern's parking lot, crossed the median and crashed head-on into the oncoming traffic.

The message seemed clear to me: I believe the Lord had interrupted our schedule that day to save our lives. So I don't become too impatient when I encounter delays.

• *There are also times when God expects us to make decisions for ourselves without His direct intervention.* When I was twelve years old, our Sunday school teacher made a sobering announcement:

"You'll be voting on me next week. I want to know if I should stay on as your teacher," Reverend Lucas explained in his raspy voice, worn from decades of preaching before his retirement. "Maybe you boys would like a younger teacher for a change. Pray much before next Sunday."

His lessons had always challenged me. I was saddened as he shuffled out of our classroom that day. My parents encouraged me to learn all the facts before voting on anything, so I didn't take the responsibility lightly.

I recalled the reasons I admired Rev. Lucas. His fervent "amens" during worship inspired me. And the stories he told of his youth were exciting—especially those of his travels throughout the West with saloon-smashing Carrie Nation. And even though I didn't understand at the time, I respected his custom of fasting one day each week.

Then I considered the effect of his retirement job as church custodian. All summer there was the sprawling church lot to mow. And each Sunday during the cold months he arose at 5 a.m., trudged a half mile to fire the furnace, and then returned home for breakfast before the hike back to Sunday school. Recalling my own distaste for shoveling coal, I reasoned he was already working much too hard to have the added burden of teaching a rowdy group of boys each week.

Still undecided, I asked my dad who pointed out the clergyman's advanced age. He also cited his problem in keeping the class quiet enough to fit the sanctity of the church. "Maybe," he observed, "it would be better to have someone else teach for a while. But you should make up your own mind."

The week passed quickly and I still felt no clear-cut guidance when Rev. Lucas handed out the small blue cards that were to serve as secret ballots. We were to vote "yes" if we thought he should stay, and "no" if we wanted a new teacher. With mixed feelings, I printed a small "no" and folded it over. Surely the ruffian he'd reprimanded just recently would vote against him too, I reasoned.

After collecting the ballots in his cupped hands, he began to open them and the class hushed expectantly. "Praise the Lord!" he exclaimed. "Twelve vote 'yes' for me to stay and only one says 'no.' How wonderful!"

I wasn't nearly as enthusiastic, realizing that I was the only dissenter. In my zeal to reach a perfect decision, I had overlooked the one thing that would have made him happiest: a unanimous vote for him to stay. A flush of embarrassment swept over me.

But Rev. Lucas beamed and added, "I'm going to keep these cards always to remind me how much you love me." This hurt even more and puzzled me as well. How could anything less than a unanimous vote please him so greatly? I wasn't to find out for several weeks.

He remained as our teacher and his ever-fresh Bible insights kept our noisy group as constrained as could be expected. But the guilt kept gnawing at me. I decided to set the matter straight. One morning before services, I called him aside and shyly confessed: "I was the one who voted 'no'—I thought you needed more rest. We were giving you such a hard time."

"I knew," he interrupted, smiling down at me and grasping my right hand in both of his. "I understood. That's what made it so special."

I'm glad Rev. Lucas sensed my true intentions that day so many years ago. His understanding reminds me of the Scripture "for the Lord seeth not as man seeth; for man looketh on the outward appearance, but the Lord looketh on the heart" (1 Samuel 16:7b).

- *In order to have our prayers answered, we must understand the significance of communion.* Some churches partake of communion (or the Eucharist) every fifth Sunday, some each quarter, some once a month, and still others each week.

In 1 Corinthians 11:23-30, we are admonished to take of the bread and the cup "in remembrance of me." But if we eat or drink unworthily, we bring judgment upon ourselves, "not discerning the Lord's body."

"For this cause, many are weak and sickly among you and many sleep," says verse 30. Paul states that many are sick and that many have actually died because they have partaken unworthily, not discerning, or understanding, what they are doing.

The bread, or wafer, represents Jesus' broken body. We are told in Isaiah 53:5b, "and with his stripes we are healed." This is verified in 1 Peter 2:24: "Who his own self bore our sins in his own body on the tree, that we, being dead to sins, should live unto righteousness: by whose stripes ye were healed." Note that "were" indicates past tense—it has already been accomplished.

If we examine ourselves carefully, ask forgiveness for our sins and understand that Christ's body was broken for our healing, as well as for our salvation, we are then in a position to receive from God.

- *We must examine our motives and purposes for desiring healing.* Why do we desire to receive a healing touch from the Master? Certainly, alleviation of pain would be a valid reason. But if our *sole* reason for praying is to be able to play golf (or any other sport) again without pain, perhaps we should place our motives under the microscope of the Spirit. Surely there should be a higher spiritual reason for physical healing.

- *There are times that we must search for God.* In Isaiah 55:6, we read, "Seek ye the Lord while he may be found, call ye upon him while he is near." Luke 24:13-32 is the account of Jesus on the road to Emmaus after His resurrection. Two of His disciples were on their way to Emmaus and they were discussing the events surrounding the Crucifixion.

Jesus drew near to them, but they did not recognize Him at first. He spoke to them and they told Him about the events of the past few days. He then explained to them all the prophecies concerning Himself. When they neared the city, "he made as if he would have gone further" (v. 28b). But at their urging, He remained with them for a while before vanishing from their sight.

Sometimes we must specifically seek the presence of Christ. We must ask Him to abide closely with us and we must make Him feel welcome. It may require extra prayer, fasting, or waiting upon Him. But it will be rewarded by a closer relationship with the Master.

CHAPTER 3

WHEN GOD WARNS US
OF THINGS TO COME

Bert, tall and robust at 72 years of age, shared with me one Sunday that he felt better than any time in the past 20 years. "If I knew what caused it, I'd do it again!" he declared.

Yet just a few weeks later, his doctors diagnosed him with a deadly blood disease. Despite the prayers of his family and church, he went to be with the Lord about two years later. Was his feeling of unusual well-being a sign from the Lord that he would soon go to be with Him? Does God alert us when He is ready to call us home?

Grandpa Walters was a perfect example of such a premonition. After my grandmother died, he quietly courted another lady. When asked why he was making so many train trips, he just grinned and replied,

"I'm going to visit relatives." He was. His new wife turned out to be a distant cousin. He fooled us.

Our trips to Virginia didn't seem quite as tiresome when I knew we would be seeing Grandpa. The smoke curling from his pipe fascinated me as he shared his views on McCarthyism and the rise of the USSR.

When his heart condition worsened, he stayed with us temporarily to be close to his doctors. Modern conveniences amazed him. He sat for hours watching our new Bendix fill with water, wash the clothes, drain, and then spin dry. He just shook his head in disbelief. I wonder how he would handle cellular telephones, VCRs, DVDs and the internet!

On the day he died, he munched on his corn flakes while I sat on the kitchen floor tying my shoes. Being a lanky lefthander, I played first base on our junior high baseball team—and that day we were planning a special trip to the adult field for practice.

When I mentioned this to Grandpa, he winked at me and announced, "I'll be over there to play with you after awhile." I looked up at my Mom in disbelief. Her expression seemed to say, *I wonder if all that medicine has clouded his mind.* We knew he couldn't walk to the baseball field. He was so ill he could barely walk to the car.

Soon after breakfast, he lay down across the bed to rest. He never got up.

We later found his shoes tucked neatly under the bed, laced and tied. He'd never done that before. Somehow he knew he wouldn't be needing them again.

Did he have a premonition of his death? I've always felt that he did.

My Wife Is Forewarned

When my wife and I married, we decided to have a short ceremony with only two witnesses in attendance. Except for the minister and the witnesses, our friend Dottie was the only person who knew our plans. Because Norma had attended college night classes with her, she had become a special Christian friend to us.

It was difficult, as years turned into decades, to watch Dottie's physical decline. After a period of hospitalization, she had been living temporarily with her daughter in a large city about two hours away. We hadn't heard from her recently, so it was disturbing when Norma experienced a startling dream about her.

Undoubtedly from the Lord, the dream pictured her many years younger, smiling broadly and attired in a baby-blue dress. The special vision was so vivid that Norma felt it was a warning from God. She took immediate action and discovered, after several inquiries, that Dottie had been hospitalized just a few miles from our home. While visiting with her that same afternoon, it became apparent to us that the Lord might be calling her home. We were able to visit twice with this cherished friend before her home-going just four days later. We are thankful for the warning God gave.

HOLY SPIRIT WARNINGS

We should never ignore the wind of the Spirit, no matter how gently His breezes waft across our lives. Just recently, I noticed that I was praying in the Spirit almost continually without conscious effort. Remembering that the Holy Spirit is our Helper, let's note these passages:

> "Likewise the Spirit also helpeth our infirmities: for we know not what we should pray for as we ought: but the Spirit itself maketh intercession for us with groanings which cannot be uttered."
>
> —Romans 8:26

> "But ye, beloved, building up yourselves on your most holy faith, praying in the Holy Ghost."
>
> —Jude 20

"Praying always with all prayer and supplication
in the Spirit."
—Ephesians 6:18a

I believe the Lord was trying to warn me of an orthopedic problem my wife would soon encounter. Had I been sensitive to the leadings of the Spirit, I could have prayed more earnestly in advance and she would have recovered even sooner. I should have taken heed, but didn't.

Soon after that, the Holy Spirit again prayed through me repeatedly. This time, I took notice and prayed with the understanding (1 Corinthians 14:15). I thought I had covered all the bases.

But a few days later, I discovered what I believed to be the purpose of the Holy Spirit's leading. My brother had been taken ill with a throat condition requiring surgery. Even though we had been un-aware of his condition earlier, the Holy Spirit knew, of course. He wanted us to begin praying for him.

The Holy Spirit not only makes us aware of impending family situations, but other important issues as well.

When we pray in the power of the Spirit, we use words given us by the Holy Spirit, rather than those from our own intellect. Thus we bypass hu-man reasoning and pray only those prayers given us from above.

I'm thankful to the Holy Spirit who prays through us even when we're too involved with other matters. He helps us and warns us of what lies ahead.

I didn't sleep well one night in 1971, just deeply enough to experience one of the most unusual and disturbing dreams of my life. I was driving along a narrow curving road in the country. On a hill to my right, I noticed two houses. One was old with dark, menacing storm clouds above it, battering it with unmerciful waves of rain. It swayed in the winds as if about to collapse.

On its left was a brand new home, all bright with a white exterior. Even though it was just next door to the older house, there was no rain or wind around it. Instead, the sun was shining brightly on it.

I didn't understand it then, but God was trying to warn me that my mom would encounter a terminal illness. The old home in my dream represented her disease-ridden body. The new home reflected a new life already in existence.

And it happened just that way about two years later. Our little son, Rick, was born exactly seven weeks after my Mom's home-going. As in the dream, his life existed before her death. But you would have to know her complete story to make sense of all this…

My Mom's Warning

Something dropped to the carpet as I leafed through Mom's old Bible. I smiled as I retrieved the small pewter cross she had treasured. It reminded her of Calvary and her miracle.

The Lord had intervened mightily in Mom's life on a sunny autumn day just a few years back. Because her encounter was so unusual, even some of her closest friends doubted her testimony …

After Dad's untimely passing, she remarried but soon divorced. She urged me and my wife to come and live with her. Mom had continued to work as a popular hairdresser before falling ill with cancer in her mid-sixties. But after radical surgery, doctors stunned her with news that she was careening toward death with only six weeks to live.

Time was short, even for someone who had already lived a full life. Undaunted, she rushed prayer requests to intercessory groups across America.

Shortly afterward, she received a surprising answer to those petitions. It came one October morning as she viewed a worship service on television. But Mom waited several days before announcing she had "something important" to share with us.

"Do you remember the white cross in the church on television last Sunday?" she began. "I was admiring it while the minister was praying for those at the altar. Just then, a little ball of bluish-white light left the cross and started speeding toward me. I know it sounds unbelievable, *but I felt it touch me.* God's love rushed through me like electricity," she declared.

"I was afraid to move or speak. The same thing happened again a few seconds later. The Lord touched me twice and now I feel twenty years younger!" Her eyes danced while she searched our faces for a reaction.

We were speechless, since we had been sitting nearby and noticed nothing amiss except that the air seemed charged with an unusual presence. Could she have imagined it? No, Mom wasn't one to exaggerate.

Then I remembered: one of the prayer requests was addressed to the church she was watching on TV that day. God had heard and answered!

The powerful shaft of light ruined her new television. Never again did it produce a clear picture despite weeks in the repair shop and examinations by the manufacturer's experts. "We've replaced everything except the chassis. Must have been a power surge," one factory rep suggested. His confusion amused Mom.

This curious phenomenon, dropping anchor

in her already-troubled life, puzzled her. Why did the Lord touch her, she questioned? Was it for healing or just a momentary oasis in the desert of pain and reality? She concluded He was granting an extension to her life and that He would be near during her illness.

Without doubt, this experience lengthened her years past the promised threescore and ten. Not surprisingly, her pain, so common in cancer patients, vanished and never returned. She perplexed her physicians by outliving their six-week forecast and enjoying a Florida vacation instead.

As Christ's love and compassion became real to her, she rededicated her tattered life. She constantly devoured her Bible and encouraged others who were ill.

Still too excited to sleep soundly, Mom awoke often at night. After tapping at our bedroom door, she would flip on our overhead lights and perch on the corner of our bed. Wide awake and radiant, she detailed her experience again and again.

We always enjoyed hearing about the incident, listening in respectful awe while rubbing sleep from our eyes. But as time passed, I reminded her we needed some rest before working the next day. She just shook her head and replied, "You don't seem to understand—*Jesus touched me!*"

When she witnessed to friends about that sacred event, some scoffed. After many stinging rebuffs, she decided she wouldn't discuss it anymore. "There's just one thing I know for certain," she sighed. "He really touched me and I'm not afraid of death anymore." Never again did she refer to the matter outside our immediate family.

The Lord had graciously given her more than two additional years to put her life in order before taking her to be with Him. On the night of her home-going, only the air conditioner's steady hum disturbed the stillness of her room.

To her nurse's surprise, she roused from semi-consciousness. Lifting her head and gazing upward, she smiled broadly as if she recognized a close Friend.

I'm sure she did.

CHAPTER 4

BEFORE THEY CALL

I'm convinced that God provides the answers to our prayers even *before* we pray in many instances. It's not a matter of begging God for an answer. He's already provided the outcome and it's just a matter of trusting Him.

I had no idea anything unusual might happen that sunny day in early September, 1974. The morning followed the usual hectic pattern of data processing departments, but I'd managed to leave the downtown bank where I worked long enough to pick up a cheeseburger and lemon freeze for lunch from the corner restaurant.

As I hurried back to the office, something occurred that was to have a far-reaching effect on the life of my family for many years to come. I heard no audible sound, but distinctly sensed a voice say-ing, *Everything will be all right.* Since I was unaware of any trouble at the time, this surprised me even though I immediately recognized the source of the prophetic words.

Both my wife and I were in good health, finan-cially stable, and experiencing no particular prob-lems. And our one-year-old, Rick, was in perfect health to the best of our knowledge.

So I inquired of the presence, "Would you mind repeating that, Lord?"

Again came the comforting words, *Ron, don't worry, everything will be all right.* He had even called me by name!

Deciding not to argue or doubt, I silently prayed, *Thank You, Lord.* At that moment, an indescribable peace surrounded me like an invisible cloud. It seemed as if the volume of the horn-honking noon-day traffic had suddenly been turned down and every distracting element was strangely far away except for the presence.

Now I understood the peace "which passeth all understanding" that Paul spoke of in Philippians 4:7. I felt as if I were literally floating instead of walking by the time I reached the back door of the bank—puzzled, but nevertheless ecstatic over the visitation I'd experienced.

A few days later, our little son visited his pediatrician for his routine one-year physical exam. We had no indication anything was amiss, but as my wife carried him out of the physician's office, I could tell by her countenance that the doctor had discovered something of a serious nature.

As soon as we reached the car, she haltingly explained, "Ron, we've got a problem—there's something wrong with his right leg. The pediatrician wants us to see a specialist."

An orthopedic surgeon immediately placed him in a brace and instructed us, "Bring him back in six weeks." Little did we realize then that the six-week interval was only a preview of what lay ahead.

Tibial torsion, causing bowlegs, was his diagnosis. It was treatable, but nonetheless wearisome for any mother who must care for a small child's needs. And think of the discomfort of the growing baby who must endure the confines of a brace during this time when he or she is most active.

When we returned to the doctor, he examined him only briefly and commented, "He's looking OK. See you again in three months!" Now we knew beyond a doubt we were destined for a long period of waiting before the problem was corrected.

While parked uptown one rainy day, I casually remarked, "Rick, Jesus is going to make your leg well someday soon." I noticed the eager look of anticipation in his young eyes, but thought my comment was more for my own encouragement, since he was probably still too young to understand. Several days later, however, when he heard my wife and me discussing his legs, he spoke up "Jeez (Jesus) make leg bett'r."

Astonished, I asked him to repeat his comment. But he just replied, "uptown," letting me know he remembered exactly when I'd made the statement.

Then I realized I'd unwittingly put myself on the spot. I was obligated to help bring about his healing. Either that or ruin his faith, I reasoned.

Although I'd been raised in a traditional Protestant church, my parents believed in divine healing and had frequently taken me to special singing and revival services at nearby full gospel churches when I was a child. So I was familiar with the principles of prayer for healing and the person of the Holy Spirit.

But the full reality of the power the Holy Spirit brings into one's life didn't strike me until after attending a Full Gospel Businessmen's meeting in October 1974. This was just a few weeks after we discovered Rick's leg problem. During prayer, I distinctly felt the electrifying presence of the Holy Spirit.

Early the next morning, I wakened suddenly to see orange and red flames dancing over the doorway to our bedroom. I vaulted out of bed, thinking Rick's room was afire. But he was sleeping soundly. I realized then that the tongues of fire I'd seen represented the presence of the third person of the godhead as recorded in Acts 2:3.

I felt it was time to put this power to work for Rick's complete healing, according to the authority Christ gave to believers in Mark 16:17-18. I explained to Rick that Jesus wanted him well, and we'd ask Him to straighten out the leg. I lifted him to my lap, laid hands on his legs, and said a short prayer. When I finished, I asked him, "Do you *really* believe Jesus will make you well?" His confident "uh-huh" displayed more faith than I felt at the moment. At any rate, my wife and I agreed his legs were beginning to look straighter now than ever before.

When it came time for his next checkup, we were both highly expectant that he would be able to junk the cumbersome braces once and for all. But the doctor, unaware of our hopes, remarked, "Some improvement this time, but he's still bowlegged. See you again in three more months." One of his doctors even talked of the possibility of surgery, since it seemed the brace wasn't accomplishing the desired results.

That night, I tried to evaluate what had happened. I asked myself why Rick hadn't been healed since God was so obviously with us in every other aspect of our lives. Where had we fallen short? Hadn't He told me months earlier it would turn out all right? And now even Rick was asking us, "Am I crippled?" undoubtedly having picked up the term from adults he'd overheard discussing his condition.

Lord, you know how weak my faith is right now, I lamented. *Please let us know that You're still with us.* I turned to a passage in the book of Nahum, though I felt there was nothing relative to our situation in the old prophetic work. Surprisingly, my attention was drawn to the prophet's words.

As I glanced through the first few verses, I was overjoyed to read, "Though I have afflicted thee, I will afflict thee no more. For now will I break his yoke from off thee, and will burst thy bonds in sunder" (Nahum 1:12-13).

God *had* heard. He would heal! We were anxious now, more than ever before, for the results of his next checkup. As he toddled down the long hallway with my wife, the doctor and I watched his legs closely. "I believe I'm going to let him out of the brace now," he observed almost dispassionately. "His legs are straight. He's supposed to be just a *little* bowlegged at his age."

As we left, he reminded us to take the brace off immediately or his legs would go too far back in the other direction. We were only too happy to remove it as we prepared to take our now-frisky son to the first available shoe store.

But even in our happiness, the doctor's parting comment was to bear upon our minds. "I want to keep a check on him every few months." Once more I petitioned the Lord to assure us that Rick was completely healed, once and for all, and that he would never have to wear the brace again. Very lovingly, I again felt the presence and heard the admonition, *You missed something the first time through in Nahum.*

I turned to the chapter again and discovered what He was now revealing to me in the ninth verse: "Affliction shall not rise up the second time." How much clearer could it be?

Lord, forgive me for doubting You, I repented. *May I never again question Your holy Word or one of Your promises.* After that day, my concern vanished since I was "fully persuaded that what He had promised, He was able to perform" (Romans 4:21).

Rick, now almost four, had his final checkup a few months later. We felt it was just a formality, since the Great Physician gave us the prognosis from His Word even before we were aware the problem existed—the day He spoke to me as I walked along the downtown streets of Knoxville.

Nevertheless, I was glad to hear Rick's voice over the telephone after he left the doctor's office. "Daddy, the doctor says I'm OK. I don't ever have to come back!" My wife came on the line and confirmed he'd been declared "perfectly normal."

Now I understand more fully the meaning of Isaiah 65:24: "And it shall come to pass, that before they call, I will answer; and while they are yet speaking, I will hear."

CHAPTER 5

FAITH THAT BRINGS RESULTS

My wife, Norma, hadn't felt well in several months. And now she had broken out in thousands of eruptions all over her body, apparently the result of a tick bite she experienced earlier. We had just left the doctor's office and arrived at the pharmacy to have them fill two prescriptions for powerful antibiotics. Since it was August, I left the motor running to give her the advantage of the air conditioning.

But when I returned only a few minutes later, I found her slumped over and unconscious. Her doctor promptly admitted her to St. Mary's Hospital—in isolation. "I'm going to treat her as if she has Rocky Mountain spotted fever," he declared in a serious tone. "Her fever is over 103."

Outside the room, he looked me straight in the eyes and told me that the next twenty-four hours would be critical. "The drugs won't begin acting for at least 24 to 48 hours," he predicted. "We'll just have to see." He seemed to have little hope for her recovery.

After some investigation, I found that Rocky Mountain spotted fever usually begins with a rash and, if not treated promptly, the patient may die even before treatment begins. Aggressive treatment is advised just as soon as a presumptive diagnosis is made.

At ten that night, I shed my gown and mask and headed home to care for our three-year-old son. I was too tired to worry. But the doctor's serious demeanor concerned me. *How did she become so ill?* I asked myself. I thought back to that spring day a few months earlier.

"Ow!"

Norma jumped up from the grass, apparently bitten on the leg by a tick of some sort. We had been watching our son play in the side yard. Later that night, she discovered that her leg was turning purple. Believing it to be nothing important, her doctor just gave her a tranquilizer the next day.

But even though the dark spot on her leg improved, she felt a little worse every day for the next three months. It was then that she had collapsed outside the pharmacy.

Near 11:00 p.m. that night, our home telephone rang. Strange, I thought, at that hour. Could Norma be worse?

It was Edna, a friend we'd invited to go with us to a gospel singing concert. When I explained our situation, she was quick to pray for my wife over the telephone. What a prayer! I had never heard a prayer like that before.

Not once did she use the phrase "if it be Thy will." She prayed as if she already knew God's will and really *expected* Him to answer. She commanded the spirit of sickness to leave Norma's body and she rebuked the fever. And she even thanked God in advance for His answer! *Rather presumptuous*, I thought at the time. We said good night and hung up. I was in a mental fog. The love of my life was critically ill and I felt helpless—except for the prayer. There was no doubt that God had prompted her to call at that exact time. Exhausted, I fell across the bed for a night of tossing and turning.

Norma, unaware of the call, moved to the bottom of the hospital bed to see if she could cool off. The next day, she told me that at the exact time Edna prayed, her fever broke and she began perspiring. The next morning, her fever was much improved, now below 100 degrees, and she was sitting on the side of the bed brushing her hair when our pastor visited her.

"Norma, what are you doing up? I heard you were in serious condition."

"Where's your faith, Rev. W?" she replied.

Later I inquired, "Surely you didn't say that to our pastor, did you?" But she did.

Later that day, I took our son Rich by to see his mom. With her still in isolation, the best we could do was park and have her wave from her window. This only made the situation worse for Rick and he burst into tears, wanting her to come home "right now."

I had an opportunity to speak with the doctor before she was released, and he seemed puzzled. "We're giving her two strong broad-spectrum antibiotics, but it couldn't have been them that broke her fever. It takes at least a day or two for them to get into the system. She's very fortunate."

God knew that I would find it difficult to properly care for a young child by myself and He had mercy on us. I will always be grateful for His compassion and healing power.

FAITH AND HOPE DEFINED

Hope, as used in the New Testament, means "earnest expectation." It means more than simply hoping it won't rain today. It means that we are constantly looking for the manifestation of the object of our hope. Faith, someone has said, means that we fully believe God will do what He has said He will do. Let's examine these two important terms.

Charles Capps, nationally known faith and end-times teacher, likens hope to a thermostat in our heating or cooling unit.[1] He says that hope is our goal setter. For instance, if we come home on a frigid afternoon and someone has mistakenly turned off the heating unit, we turn it on and set the thermostat at 70 degrees. If it is in working condition, it will work continually until the temperature in the home reaches the desired setting, and then it will cut off until the room temperature again falls below the setting. Seventy degrees is the *goal.*

But we must also have *faith* to reach the goal. Let's review the Bible definition of faith: "Now faith is the substance of things hoped for, the evidence of things not seen" (Hebrews 11:1). Romans 10:17 declares, "Faith cometh by hearing, and hearing by the word of God."

This is not the same as the *gift* of faith, spoken of in 1 Corinthians 12:9a, which is given as the Spirit wills (v. 11); this is the measure of faith which is given to every Christian as recorded in Romans 12:3.

Faith reflects the reality, or substance, of those things we hope for. So we cannot have faith unless we first have hope. And faith is the evidence of those things that are not seen (as yet). Let's look at an example. Suppose you break a tooth and have to visit your dentist. He advises you that the only way to repair the tooth is to cover it with a crown. So he deadens it, grinds away until it is the desired shape to accommodate a crown and then gives you a *temporary* crown so that you may eat properly until the dental lab provides the permanent one.

In most cases, the temporary tooth looks just as good, or better, than the old one. The temporary crown stands in the place of the permanent one, just as our faith stands as evidence of things not yet seen.

Now that we have defined faith, we should know how to activate it and put it to use in our lives. Faith is activated in two ways: by *speaking* and by *acting*.

Let's look at some biblical examples of these two principles. First, let's examine the story of the woman with the issue of blood, found in Matthew 9:20-22, Mark 5:25-34, and Luke 8:43-48. Let's review Mark's account.

And a certain woman, which had an issue of blood twelve years, and had suffered many things of many physicians, and had spent all that she had, and was nothing bettered, but rather grew worse, when she had heard of Jesus, came in the press behind, and touched his garment. For she said, If I may touch but his clothes, I shall be whole. And straightway the fountain of her blood was dried up; and she felt in her body that she was healed of that plague. And Jesus, immediately knowing in himself that virtue had gone out of him, turned him about in the press, and said, Who touched my clothes? And his disciples said unto him, Thou seest the multitude thronging thee, and sayest thou, Who touched me? And he looked round about to see her that had done this thing. But the woman fearing and trembling, knowing what was done in her, came and fell down before him, and told him all the truth. And he said unto her, Daughter, thy faith hath made thee whole; go in peace, and be whole of thy plague.

This moving story is rich in Bible truths. Let's just mention two of them at this point: (1) she took a great risk being seen out in public. According to the Levitical law, she could have been stoned for being among others during her illness. (2) The woman was "fearing and trembling." Although we don't know for certain, I believe her trembling was caused, not by fear, but by the dynamic nature of Christ's power that flowed through her body.

How did she activate her faith? First of all, she *acted* by seeking Him out and by grasping the edge of His cloak. Even before the book of James was written, she seemed to know that "faith without works is dead," and she acted accordingly (James 2:17).

Next, she had been *saying* to herself, "If I may but touch his garment, I shall be whole" (Matthew 9:21).

Note that it was not Christ's faith or the multitude's faith that brought about her healing. Christ said, "*Your* faith has made you whole."

Jairus, a ruler of the synagogue who had earlier asked the Lord to come and heal his daughter, was told by his servants at this point that she had already died and that he should not trouble the Master any further.

Hearing this negative report, Jesus immediately comforted Jairus by admonishing him, "Be not afraid, only believe" (Mark 5:36b). The Greek words for *believe* and *faith* come from the same root word *pistis*. So we can see that Christ was telling him, "Don't be afraid, just have faith."

Next, let's look at an amazing faith story from the Old Testament. Second Kings 4:8-37 gives us the story of the Shunammite woman. The village of

Shunem was located in the rolling hills of Nazareth about seven miles south of Jesus' boyhood home.

It tells of a miracle God performed through Elisha the prophet for the woman. You will remember that Elisha asked God for a "double portion" of the Spirit that rested upon Elijah. And we see from the biblical record that Elisha performed more than twice the miracles that Elijah did.

This prominent woman was prone to be generous toward Elisha. Every time he passed by her home, she served him a delicious meal. And she had an upper room built for him with a bed and furnishings where he could rest from his travels. She must have sensed by the Spirit that he was a man of God.

Elisha had his servant Gehazi speak to her and ask her if there was anything he could do for her. She declined. But Gehazi noted that they had no son and that her husband was old.

Elisha had Gehazi call her to his room and, as a sign of respect, she stood outside in the doorway and didn't enter. He told her that within a year she would have a son. And she bore that son at the time indicated by the prophet.

Some years later, the child was in the fields working with his father and he developed a severe headache. The father commanded his servants to carry him to his mother, but he soon died in her arms. Perhaps divinely directed, she placed him on Elisha's bed and shut the door.

She then asked her husband for one of his young men and a donkey so that she could travel to Elisha. Even though her husband, not knowing of his son's death, questioned her, she only answered, "It is well." She saddled a donkey and traveled the fifteen miles to Mount Carmel at top speed without stopping.

Elisha's servant ran out to meet her and ask if everything was all right. She replied, "It is well." But she went in to Elisha and caught him by the feet and told him of the situation. He ordered his servant Gehazi to take his staff and to go to the young lad and to lay the staff on his face. After doing this, there was no change. So Elisha came into the room, shut the door and prayed unto the Lord. He then lay upon the child and he became warm. He walked back and forth and then lay again on the boy, who sneezed seven times. And so he came to life and his mother took him and returned home.

As we did with the story of the woman with the issue of blood, let's see how the Shunammite woman placed her faith in action. In verses 23 and 26, she said "it is well." She spoke her faith in the present tense and did not place her faith in the future by stating "It will be well." Faith is always in the present;

the future indicates hope. Also, she spoke the desired *end result* in faith before it actually happened.

And then she went directly to Elisha because she knew he was a man of God. She didn't consult her husband or friends. Sadly, even our relatives and closest friends can be a detriment to our faith by causing doubt to come into our spirits. What would have happened if a friend had said "don't get your hopes up?" She guarded against this by speaking to no one on her journey.

She was intent on speaking the right words, and she was rewarded by having her son given back to her in good health. Speaking the wrong words, however, can keep us from realizing our hopes. Do you remember the story of the priest Zacharias and his wife Elizabeth? The angel Gabriel appeared to him at the altar and told him that his wife would conceive and bear a son to be named John.

But Zacharias doubted, citing his advanced age. Because of his unbelief, the angel rendered him speechless until after the birth of his son. No doubt the angel knew that he might negate the prophecy with his reckless words and unbelief.

Words of unbelief can have a far-reaching effect on our lives. In the mid-1970's, Norma and I were at Howard Johnson's Motor Lodge on Merchants Drive in Knoxville, attending an evangelistic service. After the sermon, the minister called for those who wanted to receive Christ and for those who would like to receive the infilling of the Holy Spirit.

A man of about thirty years of age went forward for the prayer. When the minister said "Amen," he returned to his seat near us. His wife asked, "Did you get anything?" He shook his head no. If he had realized that not all prayers are answered immediately, he could have continued believing and he would have eventually received.

"Death and life are in the power of the tongue and they that love it shall eat the fruit thereof," declares the writer of Proverbs (18:21).

Almost always it is the thoughts we entertain, the words we speak, and the actions we take beyond our "amens" that determine the outcome to our prayers.

CHAPTER 6

FOUR POWERFUL PILLARS
OF PRAYER

A local newscaster breaks into your favorite TV program and reports a vicious mountain lion loose in your community. The hair literally stands up on the back of your neck. You quickly determine that the children are all inside and you rush down to the family room to see which weapons you'll need if the ferocious animal appears on your property.

You spy a water pistol your son has left lying on the floor. Nope, that won't do at all! Next you see his BB rifle standing in the corner. Again, it's much too weak to withstand a mountain lion. You remember your 22-caliber pistol, but disqualify it as well for not being powerful enough. Your next-door neighbor owns a .357 Magnum, but you clearly would prefer your high-powered rifle for protection. So you settle on your 12-gauge speed pump, load it, and take it with you.

In much the same way, we should use the most powerful tools available to us when we are in life-and-death struggles in prayer. It doesn't make sense to repeat a weak, unstructured prayer over and over when our very lives may depend on its outcome. Nor should we depend on a formula to be successful in receiving from God. So we choose the most powerful prayer tools available to us.

They are: dynamic faith, the name of Jesus, forgiveness of those who have wronged us, and humility. Other believers may have different lists, but these are essentially the "big guns" of prayer that have worked for me.

1. Dynamic Faith

We need faith for salvation, finances, physical and emotional healing, career moves, and many other items. But just exactly what is faith? We discussed some aspects of this necessary quality in the previous chapter, but here we will explore other faith perspectives.

Simply stated, faith is that quality that enables us to believe fully what God has said in His Word.

Let's examine two Scriptures that demand strong faith. The first is found in Matthew 18:19: "Again I say unto you, That if two of you shall agree on earth as touching any thing that they shall ask, it shall be done for them of my Father which is in heaven."

This is a serious prayer principle. It cannot be used frivolously. There are three things we must understand about this type of prayer:

1. The object of the prayer should be according to the Word and must directly concern the persons who are praying. We can't, for instance, agree that the Beatles will come back together and perform a concert just for us. In other words, we can't manipulate the lives of others through prayer.
2. We must be in *agreement*. The Greek word used for *agreement* here is *sumphoneo*, which means "to sound together." It is from this word that we derive our word *symphony*.

If you are a bank teller and your computer tells you that you should have $2,522 in your drawer at the end of business, that's what you must have if you are in balance (if you are in agreement). It is not permissible to have only $2,521. That would not be in agreement.

I learned this lesson well some years ago when I became a computer programmer for a commercial bank. In writing a program to merge numeric history files on disk, I wrote a command to compare two different numeric fields to see if they were equal.

On our computer monitors, both fields reflected zeroes, but the program indicated they were unequal. Something wasn't right. After a lengthy investigation, we discovered that one of the fields indeed was zero, but the other was zero with a minus sign after it. It had previously been "minus 59 cents" and had been cleared by adding 59 to it. But it didn't erase the minus sign. *They weren't equal*, even though they appeared to be at first glance.

Agreement in prayer requires strong, immovable faith. As an example, suppose a friend asks you to agree with her that she will be chosen to be the next tenant in an apartment she desires to lease. You hear that the landlord has shown the place to another person who happens to be his first cousin. You declare, "I suppose his relative will get it for sure!" That's *not* agreement. That will negate your agreement. Remember, we must always base our prayers on God's Word, not circumstances.

To illustrate lack of agreement, suppose a friend asks you to agree with him in prayer that a severe headache will go away. You pray with him in faith and thank God in advance for removing the pain.

You then ask him if he agrees with your prayer. He replies, "I hope it'll work." Once again, that's not agreement. It won't work.

3. Since the object of this prayer is agreement, it is not necessary to repeat the prayer. We are already in agreement that God has heard us, so we should just thank and praise Him thereafter until the answer manifests itself. Other types of prayer may be repeated. It is human nature to want to pray again and again, asking God for the same thing. This is especially true if we are in a tough spot. But in this type prayer, repetition is unnecessary and it weakens our faith stance.

THE GREATEST FAITH LESSON

The second scripture contains the greatest faith lesson ever preached, which was given by Christ Himself in Mark 11. Even though it is not an example of prayer *per se*, it will produce the same results. You will remember that Christ had cursed a fig tree when He discovered that it had leaves, but no fruit. The next morning, His disciples noticed that it was dried up at the roots as they passed by. Jesus admonished them, "Have faith in God"

(v. 22). Some margins render this as "Have the faith *of* God." Continuing,

> For verily I say unto you, That whosoever shall say unto this mountain, Be thou removed, and be thou cast into the sea; and shall not doubt in his heart, but shall believe that those things which he saith shall come to pass; he shall have whatsoever he saith.
>
> Therefore I say unto you, What things soever ye desire, when ye pray, believe that ye receive them, and ye shall have them.
>
> —Mark 11:23-24

Hebrews 11:6 declares, "Without faith, it is impossible to please him." So we should note carefully this lesson which contains some of the most important words the Master spoke regarding faith. "Whosoever shall say" means just that: In certain instances, we must speak (out loud) to our problems. *This cannot be emphasized too strongly.* It's true that our relatives and friends may think we're a bit daffy, but that's not important if we're following the instructions of Christ.

We cannot be doubters and expect success with this prayer. We must fully believe with our hearts. Verse 24 summarizes this lesson: when we pray, we must believe that we receive the answers (present tense) and we will have them (future tense). Expressed another way, when we pray, we must have faith in God that allows us to believe that we've already received our answer, even though we can't see it with our human eyes. This is what allows us to praise God before the answer actually arrives.

When Christ spoke to the fig tree, it didn't wither and die immediately. But Christ didn't stand there waiting for it to dry up as proof that His prayer worked. He went about His work. He had confidence in His Father that His words would be honored.

It should be unnecessary to note again that our prayers must be in accordance with God's Word. I cannot declare, "I'm going to rob XYZ National Bank today and they will have at least $100,000 waiting for me." That's not a Christian perspective, to say the least!

Group Faith

Perhaps a few words about group faith are in order at this juncture. Full gospel and charismatic groups have been criticized in some quarters by those who believe that faith which comes about because of group dynamics is "worked up" and false. Some have described it as an "ecstatic experience."

It is certainly accurate to say that faith can rise when we are surrounded by others who are expectant for the moving of God's Spirit. Consider the emotions that drew sinners to the front in Billy Graham's giant meetings. But is that wrong? Should we chance missing the works of the Spirit because we want to appear to be quiet, reserved, and dignified?

Faith rises in group settings because of the hope and earnest expectation of those gathered together. It's very simple: did you ever have a successful pep rally in high school with only two or three in attendance? That says it all.

2. USING THE NAME OF JESUS

In the sixteenth chapter of John, Christ tells His disciples He is going away and that they should change their manner of prayer. Notice verses 23-24: "And in that day ye shall ask me nothing. Verily, verily I say unto you, Whatsoever ye shall ask the Father in my name, he will give it you. Hitherto have ye asked nothing in my name: ask, and ye shall receive, that your joy may be full."

Occasionally, we hear prayers directed to Christ rather than the Father. Or we hear "for Jesus' sake." But the proper form is to pray to the Father "in Jesus' name." It seems unlikely that God would be disappointed in us if we pray directly to Christ, but it's best to follow directions.

Why should Christ's name exact so much importance? Let's remember Paul's letter to the Philippians: "Wherefore God also hath highly exalted him, and given him a name which is above every name: that at the name of Jesus every knee should bow, of things in heaven, and things in earth, and things under the earth" (2:9, 10).

This name served Peter and John well as they were entering the temple to pray as recorded in Acts 3:6. A man who had been lame from birth lay there daily. When he saw the disciples, he asked them for alms. Peter told him, "Silver and gold have I none; but such as I have give I thee: In the name of Jesus Christ of Nazareth rise up and walk."

Then he rose up, "walking, leaping, and praising God." It seems that the name performed a double miracle here. Not only was the cripple healed, but he was immediately able to walk and leap for the first time.

The mention of the name of Jesus gets attention in heaven. Let's suppose you were on vacation, far away from your telephone and the Internet. A steward approaches you with the statement, "Your son Peter is on the telephone. You can take the call at the desk." Wouldn't you hurry to the telephone and answer his call? Of course, you would.

In much the same way, the angels of heaven come to attention when they hear the name of Jesus. And, most importantly, God Himself is attentive when He hears a prayer directed to Him in the name of His Son, Jesus Christ.

3. FORGIVING OTHERS

After delivering His great sermon on faith, Christ added something most of us wish He had left out. Let's look at Mark 11:25: "And when ye stand praying, forgive, if ye have ought against any: that your Father also which is in heaven may forgive you your trespasses."

And in Matthew 6:14-15, we are given this stern warning: "For if ye forgive men their trespasses, your heavenly Father will also forgive you: But if ye forgive not men their trespasses, neither will your Father forgive your trespasses."

Without doubt, one of the most difficult things we will ever attempt to do is to forgive those who have wronged us. Probably no one has escaped being wronged by others—many times by another Christian. It's ironic that the offender is seldom aware of the degree of hurt he or she has inflicted.

And as hard as it is to accept, our hatred and bitterness hurts only us, not the persons who have wronged us. They are getting plenty of sleep each night and we're not.

Another principle we can't ignore is, "faith worketh by love" (Galatians 5:6b). Our faith will not work for us if we are bitter toward others or if we hate them. Love and forgiveness are the catalysts that enable faith to work. As an example, suppose I have fifty pounds of cement and a pile of gravel in my driveway. I propose to repair a large hole in the pavement with these materials.

So I shovel a few bits of gravel into the crater and cover it with some of the cement. Even though it rains on the two elements, they do a poor job of fixing the orifice. Finally, I realize what I must do. I mix the cement and gravel thoroughly with water and pour the mixture into the hole. It soon becomes solid concrete. The cavity in the driveway is almost magically repaired.

Love is like the water. Without it, faith won't work. Note the startling pronouncements in 1 John 3:14-15:

> We know that we have passed from death unto life, because we love the brethren. He that loveth not his brother abideth in death. Whosoever hateth his brother is a murderer: and ye know that no murderer hath eternal life abiding in him.

And in 1 Peter 4:8, we read this strong admonition, "*Above all,* keep your love for one another at full strength, since love covers a multitude of sins" (HCSB, italics added).

What must we do? Forgive! Let it go! There will be relapses, so we must be willing to forgive anew each day. But you'll be happy to know that we're not required to invite the offenders to our house for dinner every week. They don't have to be our best friends either, but obviously we must cease hating them. Every time we have a negative thought about them, we should ask the Father to bless them that day. If we know their favorite restaurant, we can give them a gift certificate. If they enjoy flowers, we could send them a colorful bouquet and surprise them.

We can forgive in our hearts, even if there is still bitterness in our minds. Soon our pain will lessen and give way to the forgiveness bubbling up from inside. We can't forgive without love. Love's qualities are found in 1 Corinthians 13:4-7. It's a good idea to review them frequently.

And, most importantly, we should pray for our enemies as often as they come to mind. Hatred and bitterness waste tons of mental energy, and they can give us ulcers and high blood pressure. Let's take the high road of forgiveness.

My Turning Point

The turning point in my prayer life occurred when I realized I needed to ask for forgiveness from several people for things that had happened in previous years.

With a red face, I remembered a certain day when I was six years old. Three of us kids had been to the movies and we caught the bus to go home. But we paid only two fares. And when I grew up, there was a time I accepted a job ahead of another needy young man when I should have stepped aside.

And I recalled a more recent incident when I was cold and unfeeling after a company lost a large block of their business. And there were others—too embarrassing to mention.

I wrote letters to all of these, repaying them where appropriate. The slate had been wiped clean and I slept much more soundly that night. Soon, I noticed that my prayers were being answered more quickly.

Catherine Marshall, author of *Christy*, tells of such a period in her life in another of her books, *A Man Called Peter*.[1] She had been ill and incapacitated with tuberculosis for eighteen months. In September, 1944, she called and wrote letters to all she had wronged, asking for forgiveness. But her next x-rays showed no improvement.

She then realized that she had used a demanding approach to God. She relented and told Him that He could do with her whatever He wished. Feeling at peace, she retired for the evening.

During the night, Christ came to her with His healing power. She asked Him what she should do, to which He replied, "Go and tell your mother." She got up and walked to the other end of the hall and told her parents briefly what had transpired. Not wanting to disturb them further, she assured them she would explain everything in the morning.

It was no surprise that her next x-rays showed improvement for the first time. From that point on, her healing manifested slowly but surely.

4. Humility is the Key

Humility may be described as "having or showing a modest estimate of one's own importance." At the other end of the scale, we find pride, vanity, arrogance, egotism and exaggerated self-esteem.

For ease in discussing humility, we will use pride as one of its opposites. At the outset, we should understand that human pride is never completely conquered. It is a daily struggle—it keeps peeking out from our attention-starved psyche.

But there are definite advantages to overcoming this sinister trait of character. A pastor who has observed God's working among the sick observes that the healing of physical illness most often comes to the humble person, rather than one who is prideful.

In Numbers 12:3, Moses is described as "very meek (humble) above all the men which were upon the face of the earth." But he was the person most used by God in his generation. We are given a solemn warning about the dangers of pride in Proverbs 6:16-17: "These six things doth the Lord hate: yea, seven are an abomination unto him: A proud look, a lying tongue and hands that shed innocent blood." God places pride in the same category as liars and murderers!

Let's list a few of the items that can reflect pride in our lives. Topics 1-8 are adapted from the video series "Humility, Key to Greater Grace."[2] Topic 9 and all comments are the author's.

1. Pride is always speaking of itself to impress others. It promotes itself in the form of bragging.

2. Prideful people always want to be noticed right away and they are irritated if ignored. If they walk into a meeting already in progress, they expect the speaker to stop and introduce them. If they enter a retail store to make a

purchase, they expect to be acknowledged immediately. We all know this is not always possible in today's world. The humble individual isn't angered by an occasional delay.

3. Pride is not easily impressed by the accomplishments of others. If a friend comments on nice hotel facilities while on vacation, a proud person might counter with, "But you should have seen *ours*. Jennifer Lopez stayed in our room once."

4. Pride causes us to be poor listeners. If we are plagued by pride, we are always thinking about our next comment and we fail to show the proper respect for what others are trying to tell us.

   Studies have shown that people who constantly interrupt others while conversing have a higher incidence of cardiovascular disease. This is true even if the person's blood pressure, cholesterol, and triglycerides are well controlled.

5. Humility asks first; pride assumes and interrupts. For example, suppose you telephone a friend at work. An arrogant person assumes his or her business is more important than the worker's task at the moment. So they launch into their discussion without regard to the time constraints of the listener.

A humble person would first ask, "Do you have time to talk with me a minute?"

6. Pride bluffs; humility says "Sorry, I don't know."

7. Pride makes us unthankful; if we are full of pride, we feel as if we deserve benefits without thanking others for them. In other words, we feel above saying "Thank you" for kindnesses.

8. If we are afflicted by pride, we don't want to be corrected. We feel as if our way is the only right way and that we know more than any person who would dare criticize us.

9. "You ought to" or "you should have" are frequent suggestions from prideful persons. They wrongly feel they always know what is best for others without being aware of all the details.

Humility is a condition of the heart and mind so it isn't necessarily reflected on the outside. A person can drive a 30-year-old automobile and live in a one-room shack without having an atom of humility. Conversely, one can live in a mansion, drive a different luxury car each day of the week and still be humble.

Let's not judge one another, but remember Peter's warning in 1 Peter 5:5b: "Be clothed with humility: for God resisteth the proud, and giveth grace to the humble."

Perhaps the golden example of humility was that of our Lord in John 13:1-17. Knowing that His death was near, He bent down and washed His disciples' feet, including those of His betrayer, Judas. It is hard to imagine a greater example of love and humility.

CHAPTER 7

EIGHT ESSENTIALS OF ANSWERED PRAYER

In addition to the Four Powerful Pillars of Prayer discussed in the previous chapter, there are eight other essentials we must practice to realize the most from our prayer requests. They are: praise, thanksgiving, worshipping the Master, expectancy for the answer, the giving of tithes and offerings, consistency in our Christian life, "Touch Not God's Anointed" and the prayer of relinquishment.

1. PRAISE

Praise is often overlooked or given minor standing in our prayer lives, but it is an integral part of talking with God. The Scriptures are replete with references to its value. Here are just a few:

> "But thou art holy, O thou that inhabitest the praises of Israel."
>
> —Psalm 22:3

God lives within our praises. It just makes sense to include sincere praise as part of our prayers.

> "Rejoice in the Lord always: and again I say, Rejoice."
>
> —Philippians 4:4

> "Rejoice evermore."
>
> —1 Thessalonians 5:16

> "I will bless the Lord at all times: His praise shall continually be in my mouth."
>
> —Psalm 34:1

> "By him therefore let us offer the sacrifice of praise to God continually, that is, the fruit of our lips giving thanks to his name."
>
> —Hebrews 13:15

Raymond T. Richey, well-known healing evangelist of the early 20th century, was born in 1893. While still a young man, his eyesight failed because of an injury. But in 1911, his eyes were healed as the result of prayer. Soon afterward, he became a Christian but contracted tuberculosis. He was later healed of this deadly malady also.

During World War II, he purchased a giant tent with red, white, and blue stripes. He then held tent meetings for the members of the armed forces and saw many saved and healed.[1]

In his book, *The Name of Jesus*[2], Kenneth E. Hagin describes an incident in Richey's life that emphasized the importance of praise after praying the prayer of agreement.

Both Hagin and Richey attended a convention in a large church where the pastor had just suffered a heart attack. The doctors told his wife that he was dying, so she rushed to the telephone and called the leaders of the convention to pray.

There were approximately 2,900 persons in attendance. About 2,100 were seated in the main auditorium and approximately 800 in an overflow room. Raymond Richey was called to the podium to lead in prayer. All lifted their hands and prayed in the name of Jesus for his healing. Everyone prayed at once. As the voices ceased one by one, Brother Richey asked, "How many of you believe God heard us?"

At least 90 percent of the crowd lifted their hands. Richey then said, "Let's lift our hands and praise God for the answer." Everyone lifted their voices in praise. As the sounds of praise trailed off, Richey left the platform and the song leader returned. But Richey suddenly whirled around and climbed the stairs to the podium again.

He asked the crowd, "How many of you are going to keep praying for Brother S.?" About 90 percent of the people lifted their hands. Richey said, "What for? I thought you already believed God heard you."

Most of the crowd missed his meaning; many just blinked their eyes in confusion. Richey was trying to remind them that additional prayer wasn't necessary if they really believed that God had heard them the first time; it was continued praise that would bring about the answer.

The minister recovered and served God for many more years. No doubt it was those who fully believed God and offered their praises that helped bring about his healing.

2. Thanksgiving

The giving of thanks is just as important as praise. In Ephesians 5:20 we find these words: "Giving thanks always for all things unto God and the Father in the name of our Lord Jesus Christ." And in 1 Thessalonians 5:18, Paul tells us, "In every thing give thanks: for this is the will of God in Christ Jesus concerning you."

In Luke 17:12-19, we are given the account of ten lepers who asked Jesus to have mercy on them. He told them to go and show themselves to the priest. This was ordinarily done only after a person recuperated so that the priest could certify him as healed before he again entered society.

As they went their way, all were cleansed. But one of the lepers, seeing that he was healed, "with a loud voice" glorified God. He returned and fell on his face at Jesus' feet and thanked Him. Jesus told him, "Thy faith hath made thee whole." Not only was he cleansed, he was made whole. The flesh that had rotted off his body was restored. Should we then doubt the value of giving thanks unto God?

3. WORSHIPPING THE MASTER

To praise is to express approval or admiration. Worship is related to praise, but it is not the same. Worship shows intense love or admiration for Deity.

In Matthew 15:22-28, we find the story of a woman of Canaan who touched the heart of Christ when she worshipped Him and asked for His help. She had been begging Him for help because her daughter was vexed with a devil. But He "answered her not a word." His disciples even wanted to send her away. Christ told her that He was sent only to the Jews, but she worshipped Him and again begged for His help.

She could well have taken offense when He called her a "dog" in verse 26, but she continued to seek His mercy. "Then Jesus answered and said unto her, 'O woman, great is thy faith: be it unto thee even as thou wilt.' And her daughter was made whole from that very hour" (v. 28).

Genuine, heartfelt worship touches the heart of the Great Physician.

4. Be Expectant for the Answer

As a youngster, I was interested in binoculars and telescopes. The prospect of viewing craters on the moon and seeing Saturn's rings intrigued me. Our mailbox was frequently filled with advertisements from optical firms. One such company, Edmund Salvage Company (later Edmund Scientific Corporation) in Barrington, New Jersey, had a special offer that appealed to a non-rich lad such as I.

For only a dollar, one could purchase a kit of eight lenses that had small imperfections such as bubbles or chips. Some were condensing lenses and some were magnifiers. My imagination worked overtime as I planned the telescopes I could make with this inexpensive kit. When I mailed the order, I sat down with a calendar and plotted the approximate day I would receive my optics.

The day before the expected arrival, I was waiting for the mailman on the front steps, just in case. And I was there every day thereafter. Not too many days afterward, the coveted package arrived. It was everything I had expected and I derived many hours of pleasure from it.

I was *hoping* that the package would arrive each day. The New Testament word for hope is *elpis,* Greek for "favorable and confident expectation." I expected the optics at any time.

Bible hope and everyday hope are quite different. We may say, "I hope it doesn't rain today." But that's not a confident expectation; it's merely a desire or wish. True Bible hope is confidently expecting and always looking for the answer to a prayer as if it were just around the corner.

For instance, suppose two persons are anointed with oil and hands are laid on them for healing. One of them wants to "wait and see" if anything happens. It usually doesn't with this approach.

The other may "confidently expect" to receive his or her healing immediately. He will be watchful for any change for the better. This type of vibrant faith and expectancy is fertile soil for the healing anointing of Christ to do its work.

Another consideration is imperative for those standing in faith for their answers. We must keep our faith strong after prayer, no matter what the circumstances seem to indicate.

Do you remember how faith is activated? Faith is ignited by *words* and *actions*. Consider this situation that contains destructive words: You have just received prayer for whiplash pain. A friend asks you if your pain is better and you reply, "No, it's about the same." Such a negative confession may cancel out any healing power that was imparted. A better answer, still truthful, would have been "I believe I have received my healing."

We may want to *act* in faith after prayer. However, there could be a danger here. We should not act in a manner that is not approved by our physician. It would be unsafe, for instance, for a diabetic to throw away his medication before his doctor consents. We should act in faith, but within the limits of good sense.

5. God's Tithes and Offerings

A definite sore spot with many Christians is the tithe, or tenth, of their income. Perhaps the most familiar Scripture on tithing is found in Malachi 3:8-11. It is downplayed by some because it appears in the Old Testament. But we find several references to giving in the New Testament, such as Luke 6:38: "Give, and it shall be given unto you; good measure, pressed down, and shaken together, and running over, shall men give unto your bosom. For with the same measure that ye mete withal it shall be measured to you again."

Persons who consistently live a life of tithing and giving to the Lord find that their remaining 90% spreads further than 100% of "untithed" funds. Giving can be compared to a drain pipe in your house. If the drain is clogged, the flow is interrupted. Likewise, if we don't give, our "receiving pipe" is obstructed and there is no room for God to give back to us.

Remembering that God freely and lovingly gave His only begotten Son for us (John 3:16), there are at least three things we should freely give back unto Him: our time, our love, and a tenth of our increase. I was well into adulthood before I realized that God is not stingy with us and that we shouldn't be close-fisted with Him.

Some years ago, we were about to board a plane for a vacation at the beach. A white-knuckle flight? No way—this was vacation!

As our jet roared away from Knoxville, my wife and our now seven-year-old, Rick, eagerly scanned the sunny Tennessee hills below. We were looking forward to Florida's sand, surf, and sunshine. But some disturbing words in our breakfast conversation kept nagging at me until I was too preoccupied to think about the beach.

After eating, Rick asked if he could buy another sweet roll to take along. We agreed—if he would pay with the twenty dollars we'd given him for spending money.

"I still have more than nineteen dollars left!" he announced after making his purchase, as if trying to convince himself the meager sum would last the entire trip.

Even though I didn't understand why, his comment troubled me on the inside. Did he really think we would limit his vacation spending to a fixed amount?

The idea hurt deeply.

Didn't he realize we would provide whatever he needed, even if it exceeded what we'd originally given him? The thought continued to bother me even after returning home, although he spent far more than the $20!

Why would such a small matter concern me so greatly, I wondered? I recalled a familiar passage from the story of the prodigal son that expressed my feelings exactly: "Son, thou art ever with me, and all that I have is thine" (Luke 15:31b).

That's precisely how I felt about Rick. Surely we humans must love our children in much the same way that God loves us, I concluded. If *we're* offended when accused of being stingy, how much more it must sadden our heavenly Father to be charged unjustly!

Had I ever grieved Him in the same way, by assuming He places penny-pinching limits on the gifts He provides? I was almost certain I had. I knew how much we enjoyed providing for our own son, but then I realized God loves His children far more than we can ever love ours and He delights in giving us good gifts if we ask him (Matthew 7:11).

I'm glad Rick voiced his thoughts that day. It's helped me understand more clearly God's boundless love for His children and to realize His blessings are limitless, and freely given.[3]

A New Task

In October 1977, I was preparing to get on the elevator where I worked as EDP auditor for a large bank. I was startled to hear the Lord's voice saying to me, "I have a new task for you to perform." For the previous six years, my wife and I had operated "Devotions for Shut-Ins." We had an extra telephone line installed at our home where we prepared recorded messages each day consisting of religious music, Scriptures, and short sermons.

We had numerous calls from shut-ins and nursing home residents. Just before the Lord spoke to me, it seemed as if most of our callers "vanished." Some recovered and returned home, some moved, and some died. No doubt this new task, whatever it might be, would take the place of our telephone devotions.

A definite possibility was the completion of my college degree. I had been thinking about returning to college, but agonized about the financial aspect. How would I provide for my family if I quit my job? And would I be able to obtain another job, even with a college degree, at age 40?

Shortly afterward, I attended a meeting of the Full Gospel Businessmen's Fellowship. While we were praying for the needs of others, a lady to my right stood and began prophesying: "Do what I have commanded you to do; I will uphold you and I will provide for you. Do not be afraid." I remember two things about that prophecy: I felt it was directed to me and the lady was dressed in a white outfit. Nothing more. As far as I know, I was not acquainted with her, nor have I seen her since.

The next summer, I resigned my position and enrolled in the University of Tennessee. On my last day of work, I was presented with a check representing my funds in the 401(k) plan. To my surprise, it was double what I had anticipated. Apparently I was vested without knowing it. After two years of additional studies, I graduated and quickly found employment.

While at my new job on a particular day, I was bombarded with thoughts that I should send an anonymous cash gift to the parents of a terminally ill little girl. After several hours of persuasion by the Holy Spirit, I gave in and withdrew a modest sum of money from our savings and sent it to the family. It enabled them, even though beset with overwhelming medical bills, to give their child a wonderful last Christmas.

When checking our mailbox that very night, I found a check payable to me from the publisher of a monthly banking publication. It was payment for an article I had sent them months before. The amount? Exactly the amount of the money we had sent the sick girl's family.

A gentleman shared the following story with me: The Holy Spirit kept bringing to his mind a retired widow who had only a small government check each month. He anonymously sent her a sum of cash and promptly forgot it. Just a few weeks later, he was attending the annual meeting of a financial organization. When they conducted a drawing, his was the second name picked. The amount he won?

You guessed it—the exact amount he had earlier sent to the widow!

The Widow of Zarephath

During a famine, Elijah dwelt by the Brook Cherith. He drank from the brook and the ravens brought him food, but the brook soon dried up because of lack of rain. And the Lord told him to go to Zarephath where a widow would provide for him.

When he arrived, he saw the widow gathering sticks. He asked her to get him a drink of water. As she was going to get it, he also asked her to bring him some bread to eat. She told him that all she had was a little meal and oil and that she was going to prepare it for herself and her son. After that, they had nothing and would die, she said.

Elijah told her not to be afraid and to go and do as she had said. But he wanted her to make him a little cake first. Even though she faced starvation, she did as the man of God asked her. She gave as unto the Lord *first* and the Lord provided food for them "for many days."

King David also found the secret to successful giving. He declared he would give nothing unto the Lord "which doth cost me nothing" (2 Samuel 24:24). Both King David and the widow of Zarephath gave things of significant value.

Here are some points to remember in our giving to the Lord:

a. Give to worthy causes (such as your church); "sow into good ground."

b. Give without fanfare. "That thine alms may be in secret and thy Father which seeth in secret himself shall reward thee openly" (Matthew 6:4).

c. Don't attach conditions to your gifts; give them unconditionally. Give to causes where there is no possibility of being repaid. In other words, "don't give to get."

d. Don't rush God; crop growth takes time. Don't despair before the harvest. Ecclesiastes 11:1 declares, "Cast thy bread upon the waters: for thou shalt find it after many days."

Tithing and giving have been linked to the term *prosperity*. Due to abuses by some, prosperity has also become synonymous with a lifestyle of extravagance. But the true meaning of prosperity is abundance, not extravagance. To me, abundance means always having enough for our needs.

God is faithful to provide for us when we are consistent in our giving to Him.

6. CONSISTENCY IN THE CHRISTIAN LIFE

The dictionary defines *consistency* as "conformity with previous practice." In Luke 4:16, we read that Christ went into the synagogue on the Sabbath day "as his custom was." He was *consistent* in His practice of worshipping God. His Father knew He could count on Him to be there on the Sabbath and on the holy days.

God places great value on our consistency in worshipping and serving Him. This includes our prayer lives, study of the Scriptures, tithing, and the words we speak: words of faith or words of unbelief. Joshua and Caleb returned from the Promised Land with a report of faith. The remaining ten spies brought back "an evil [unbelieving] report." Of the twelve, only Joshua and Caleb were privileged to enter the Promised Land.

Many busy Christians find that a "daily Bible" helps them to be consistent in Bible study. Members of the Faith Life Church in Branson, Missouri, are encouraged to read a chapter from the Bible each day, Monday through Friday. They attest to the fact that it strengthens them in their walk with Christ.

When God is certain He can depend on us, He may surprise us by the assignments He entrusts to us. Consider the following true story.

❧

"Pray for Charlie!"

Hearing those words in my spirit, I roused from sleep and squinted at the clock. Five a.m.! Right on the dot. I suspected it was the Lord and asked, "What did You say?"

"Pray for Charlie!" There was an urgency in the command.

I had only one close friend by that name. He was a wonderful Christian who was a tireless worker in our Sunday school class. Not having a regular piano player in our class, he was always willing to "haunt" the other classes and ask their pianists to come and play our old upright for a couple of songs. And at Christmas, he almost single-handedly put together the fruit baskets we delivered to the nursing home. As far as I knew, he was well and having no problems.

What could be wrong? I wondered. I had no clue. Nonetheless, I prayed. It was several days later that we found out he was facing open heart surgery at that very moment. He underwent the procedure, recovered in a short time, and went on to live many more productive years.

Why would God wake me up and ask me to pray? I asked myself. Couldn't He just as easily have watched over Charlie and his surgical team without my involvement?

Yes, but I would be overjoyed knowing that the Lord had wakened even my worst enemy and asked him to pray for me. Perhaps He already has done so—and they just haven't told me. I question no more.

7. "Touch Not God's Anointed"

In Psalm 105:15 we are warned, "Touch not mine anointed, and do my prophets no harm." These were the kings and priests that God had anointed for His work. Today, this would apply to ministers, evangelists, etc. which God has anointed.

The Hebrew word for "touch" is *naga,* which means to strike or smite violently. This would include criticism, lies and gossip aimed at the man of God. Here's an example that I've heard with some frequency:

"What do you think of Rev. X on television?"

"I believe he's a fake. And those people are faking when they fall down when he touches them. I believe he pays them."

God is very sensitive when it comes to criticism of His ministers. Who are we to criticize another's servant? We may not know all the details. In fact, we seldom do.

I've been aware of several situations in life where ministers have been criticized and mistreated without cause. And I've noticed an amazing correlation between these events and troubles that come in the lives of those who have wounded His ministers.

The message is very clear: Let's pray for our ministers, treat them as we would want to be treated, and cease all criticism. If they need chastising, God will see to it.

8. RELINQUISHMENT - THE ULTIMATE PRAYER

Webster defines *relinquishment* as "giving up or letting go." The prayer of relinquishment simply means that we subordinate our will to the will of God. Perhaps this was best illustrated by Christ in the Garden of Gethsemane after praying earnestly and sorrowing greatly. He said, "O my Father, if this cup may not pass away from me, except I drink it, thy will be done" (Matthew 26:42b).

You probably remember the name Nathaniel Hawthorne from a high school or college literature course. Hawthorne, who lived in the early nineteenth century, was well known for *The Scarlet Letter* and *House of Seven Gables.*

While in Rome in 1860, his oldest daughter, Una, became gravely ill with malaria. The doctor informed Una's mother that she would die unless her fever broke before morning. Her mother sat by her bed on this moonless night and thought, *I cannot …cannot bear this loss.* Then her thinking changed suddenly and she reasoned that she should not doubt God's goodness. If He wanted to take Una, she would fight no longer.

At that moment, her heart was unburdened and she felt a strange peace and happiness she hadn't felt since the start of her daughter's illness. Within just minutes, she felt Una's brow and it was cool and moist. The fever had miraculously been broken and the girl recovered.[4]

Yes, there is a definite place for the prayer of relinquishment. And it indicates surrender to God and His ultimate goodness.

CHAPTER 8

PRAYER CLOTHS AND ANOINTING WITH OIL TODAY

An ulcer?!" I couldn't believe it.

"That's right, you have a small, non-obstructive pre-pyloric ulcer. I'm giving you three prescriptions and a diet plan. You can leave the hospital today." Dr. B. acted as if he had had hundreds of cases like this before. But I was only nineteen. Did teenagers get ulcers?

Since I was off from work for two weeks, I had ample time to think. What could have caused this illness? True, I had just taken my first full-time job. And it didn't give me much peace of mind when my supervisor, unprovoked, threw a chair at me. So I just took the tranquilizers, four per day, and swilled down an antacid every few hours to stop the burning pain in my stomach.

But the ulcer didn't heal and I was in pain for six years. Then came a breakthrough. One night I dreamed that a tall, dark-haired man came and prayed for me. In the dream, my stomach stopped hurting after his prayer. The dream was so vivid that I remembered it and wondered who the tall man could be.

Just a few weeks later, T. L. Lowery, a well-known evangelist of the Church of God (Cleveland, TN) came to our area for a revival. Seeing him for the first time, I noted that he looked exactly like the man in my dream.

One particular night, I was unable to attend services. But my mom went through the prayer line at the end of that service. In addition to asking prayer for her own physical needs, she told Brother Lowery about my illness. He asked if she had a handkerchief. She produced one that had a bouquet of red and lavender flowers embroidered at one edge and handed it to him. He prayed over it and told her to have me carry it with me.

Within just a few days, my symptoms subsided and I have never had trouble with ulcers since. (And I still have the embroidered handkerchief.) Is there a biblical basis for what we now term "prayer cloths"? Let's review the passage in Acts 19:11-12:

"God was performing extraordinary miracles by Paul's hands, so that even facecloths or work aprons that had touched his skin were brought to the sick, and the diseases left them, and the evil spirits came out of them." (HCSB)

It seems that cloth stores the power of God. Tradition tells us that other cities wanted Paul to visit them and to pray for their illnesses. Since he was unable to go immediately, he sent cloths that had come into contact with his body.

Some people criticize the distribution of prayer cloths, but anointing with oil has maintained acceptance through the years. Let's look at James 5:14-15:

"Is any sick among you? let him call for the elders of the church; and let them pray over him, anointing him with oil in the name of the Lord: And the prayer of faith shall save the sick, and the Lord shall raise him up; and if he have committed sins, they shall be forgiven him."

Some later translations, such as the Holman Christian Standard Bible, specify "olive oil." Even some mainline denominations still use this means of prayer.

In Mark 6, Christ sent out His disciples two by two. "And they went out, and preached that men should repent, And they cast out many devils, and anointed with oil many that were sick, and healed them" (vv. 12-13).

Thus we see that anointing with oil was not unusual in Bible times. The Roman Catholic Church administers the Sacrament of Extreme Unction when a person is ill and not expected to live. Since Vatican II, this has been known as "anointing of the sick."

The word *sick* in James 5:14 is translated from the Greek word *astheneo,* which means weak or feeble, or beyond helping oneself. The term "prayer of faith" in verse 15 emphasizes the fact that it is not the oil, a symbol of the Holy Spirit, that heals. It is prayer, literally bathed in faith, that does the work.

What, then, is the need for the oil? No doubt we've all heard the term "point of contact." The oil reminds us of the presence of the Holy Spirit. And it enables us to establish the exact time when we receive our healing, even though the full manifestation may come a bit later.

One of the most dramatic illustrations I've heard of a point of contact was related by the late Kenneth E. Hagin.[1] In this case, it was the "amen" at the end of the prayer that served as his point of contact.

He tells of the time when, as a teenager in McKinney, Texas, he was healed of a condition that resembled Bell's palsy where the facial muscles are paralyzed. One Monday morning, he awakened to find that the right side of his face was "dead." It was difficult for him to talk, smile, or to close his eyelid when he tried to sleep.

He decided to go down to the full gospel tabernacle on Wednesday evening and ask for prayer. The service ran late and Brother Conner was about to dismiss the crowd with a brief prayer. But Hagin lifted his hand and asked for prayer for his healing. He walked to the front of the auditorium and Brother Conner anointed him with oil and prayed.

Hagin said he didn't hear the prayer, because he was waiting for the "amen." That was the point at which he would start believing he was healed, based upon Romans 4:17b: " ...and calleth those things which be not as though they were." The moment the pastor said "amen," Hagin shouted in faith, "Thank God, it's gone!"

After the service was dismissed, several members who heard his exclamation asked him if he was healed, telling him that he didn't look any different. But Hagin explained, "Faith doesn't go by looks or feelings; 'faith is the evidence of things not seen.'"

Several young people walked with him, including his girlfriend, as they headed home. As they passed under a street light, he laughed and they noted that his mouth was still twisted. "Are you feeling any different?" they asked.

"No," he replied.

"Then why do you think you're healed?"

"I don't *think* it, I *know* it."

His girlfriend invited him inside when they reached her house. As Hagin explains, both she and her mother were short ladies. They placed him under a light and looked at his face. This caused him to laugh again, which made his mouth look even worse. His girlfriend told her mother, "He thinks he's healed."

"No," he replied, "I don't think it, I *know* it."

Her mother wisely observed, "Maybe Kenneth knows something about faith that we don't know."

The next morning, all of his symptoms had disappeared. His girlfriend exclaimed, "You're healed!"

Hagin replied, "Yes, I was healed last night when Brother Conner anointed me with oil."

He was "calling those things which be not as though they were," and it resulted in his healing.

CHAPTER 9

PRAYING WITH THE SPIRIT

"Praying always with all prayer and supplication in the Spirit."

—Ephesians 6:18

The Holy Spirit is still somewhat of a mystery to many Christians. He is often thought of as a ghost or as a mystical unseen presence. Some even feel that manifestations of the Spirit are of the devil. But the third Person of the Godhead is very real. He is described as being seven dimensional in the Amplified Bible: Comforter, counselor, helper, advocate, intercessor, strengthener, and standby (John 16:7).

He is our comforter and counselor. As such, He will often speak to us. Many times, it will be just a leading or a "nudge." He is always gentle and will not force Himself on us. At other times, He will speak to us in a still, small voice. Sometimes His voice is so forceful that it seems almost audible.

He is also our helper. Have you ever tried to assemble a bookcase by yourself? It's just not possible to hold a heavy wooden shelf in one hand and be six feet away to insert the end into the upright plank at the same time. A helper doesn't actually *do* the job for us, he *helps* us. This is the nature of the Holy Spirit.

Jesus said "he dwelleth with you, shall be in you" (John 14:17). The Holy Spirit abides within each believer, but Christ was speaking of the day when all His disciples would be filled with the Holy Spirit as recorded in Acts 2:4.

In 1 Corinthians 12, Paul lists nine gifts of the Holy Spirit: the word of wisdom, the word of knowledge, faith, gifts of healing, working of miracles, prophecy, discerning of spirits, divers kinds of tongues, and the interpretation of tongues. We often see manifestations of the word of knowledge in the Christian media today, but the subject of tongues seems to attract the most attention and comment. Perhaps this is because it is so unusual.

It is at this juncture that many believers are thrown off track. They believe that *tongues* refers to someone suddenly standing up in church and shouting in an unknown language. While this does happen, the majority of speaking in tongues is what is referred to as "devotional tongues," more commonly known as a "prayer language." It can be started or stopped at will and is always within the control of the person praying.

So we can identify two types of tongues: one which is to be spoken out in church when an interpreter is present (1 Corinthians 14:27-8) and another, devotional tongues, when a believer is speaking only to God in private and not to the church (1 Corinthians 14:2). This is prophesied in Isaiah 28:11, "For with stammering lips and another tongue will he speak to this people."

The Holy Spirit is our intercessor. In Romans 8:26-27, we are reminded that we don't always know exactly how to pray. But the Holy Spirit knows and He makes "intercession for the saints according to the will of God."

In Luke 24:49, Christ told His disciples to wait in Jerusalem until they were "endued with power from on high." This promise was fulfilled on the Day of Pentecost.

Is this experience necessary for salvation? No, but it gives us greater power to witness to others and to serve God. I recall the night I received the infilling of the Holy Spirit. Or should I say "morning"? I was awakened suddenly at 2:00 a.m. and even though

I'm usually a sleepyhead, I was immediately alert with no accompanying drowsiness.

I sensed a presence at my side. And then I felt God's love being poured out upon me. It felt as if an electrical current was charging my body, starting at the top of my head. It moved downward slowly—very slowly, until it reached my feet. The next night, the very same thing happened again at precisely the same time. The Holy Spirit had visited me twice.

Your experience will be different. But it is still normal for us to ask, "How can I receive the infilling of the Holy Spirit?" First, we are told to *ask* of God (Luke 11:13). Next, we should observe the New Testament *method* used in receiving the Holy Spirit. In Acts 8:17, Peter and John traveled to Samaria. They prayed for the Samaritans, laying their hands on them, and they received the Holy Spirit. In Acts 19:6, Paul laid his hands on some disciples in Ephesus and they also received the Holy Spirit and spoke with tongues.

After asking God for the infilling of the Spirit, you can call upon a Spirit-filled believer to pray and lay hands on you. You may or may not experience the Holy Spirit praying through you immediately. But remain yielded to the Spirit and your prayer language will manifest itself as He wills. After you are filled with the Holy Spirit, He will be able to pray through you according to the perfect will of God.

CHAPTER 10

DEALING WITH THE DECEIVER

A s early as Genesis 3:1, we learn that Satan is a deceiver. And he still walks about "seeking whom he may devour" (1 Peter 5:8b).

Regrettably, we must expect him to challenge our happiness while we are here on the earth. It's not unusual, then, for this scoundrel to try to steal the answers to our prayers. This is especially true if we receive answers that are mainly attributable to another's prayers in our behalf.

Why should this be? If, for instance, we receive physical healing solely as the result of our pastor's prayers, we are not as involved in the process as we would have been had we prayed alone. Perhaps, because of intense pain and fatigue, we've laid the total burden for our healing on him. Therefore, it may be that we don't value God's healing touch as highly as we should. Or it could be that we don't continue in praise and thanksgiving, thinking that "it's done." This is when the deceiver goes into action.

Let's suppose that, after prayer at your church, you receive healing from the Lord for a very painful lower-back condition that has bothered you continually for many years. For about five weeks, you are completely free of pain and stiffness. Then, without warning, you scream aloud as you experience a stabbing pain in your lumbar area.

Having been in pain for so many years, it is *normal* for you to reason, *I thought I was healed, but I suppose it's come back*." But the correct response would be, "I have been completely well for five weeks; I know I'm healed. Satan, take your symptoms and leave now, in Jesus' name!" The Scriptures assure us that if we resist the devil, he will flee from us (James 4:7b).

Fear always opposes our faith. "For God hath not given us the spirit of fear; but of power, and of love, and of a sound mind" (II Timothy 1:7). Fear, I've found, can be crippling.

When I was a teenager, my mom underwent major surgery. I waited alone in the hall, wondering how things were progressing. A few minutes into her procedure, an orderly raced out of the surgery suite and frantically pounded on the elevator buttons until an elevator picked him up. Soon, he returned with a pint of blood and raced back into the surgical area. I was paralyzed with fear. Was the blood for her and would she live? Yes, the blood was for her, and I'm happy to say she recovered nicely.

Just a few years back, I became aware of a bothersome cyst on my upper back. It gave me no particular problem, but it became infected and the dermatologist drained it, instructing me to set up a thirty-minute surgery when it healed. Reporting for the office surgery on the appointed day, a technician informed me that its appearance had changed and that they wanted to do a biopsy to be certain it wasn't malignant.

As I left the office that day, fear tried to paralyze me. On the elevator, I quietly repeated the words, "I will not be afraid. I will not be afraid." And the fear left. I'm embarrassed to say that I was surprised that it vanished so easily. Within a few days, the test results came back negative.

Also consider the story of Kellie Copeland's daughter, Lyndsey. On Christmas Day, 1995, 11-year-old Lyndsey suddenly became ill with an aggressive case of meningitis. Many times, this fast-acting disease isn't diagnosed until the child is near death. Even if it is recognized and treated with antibiotics, they frequently don't take effect until it is too late. Lyndsey exhibited flu-like symptoms on

Christmas Eve and felt so badly that she didn't feel like opening presents the next morning.

Early that same afternoon, she became delirious and her doctor ordered her to the emergency room. By the time she arrived, she was unconscious. The doctor announced that a spinal tap revealed meningitis. Her mother Kellie remembers, "As soon as the doctor spoke those words, I felt as if someone had thrown a blanket of fear over me."[1]

Not answering the doctor, Kellie turned and went out into the hall. Her sister, just arriving, asked, "What is it?" Instead of answering, Kellie felt there was something she must do first. She resolutely stated, "I refuse fear. Jesus, there is blood between me and You over Lyndsey. I have a covenant!"

She had daily been pleading the blood of Jesus over her family. The fear evaporated.

About 3:30 that afternoon, the doctor started Lyndsey on strong antibiotics, warning the family not to get their hopes up. "These antibiotics take at least 24 to 48 hours to have any kind of effect," he warned. "Children who have contracted meningitis usually die before 24 hours have passed."

At that point, Lyndsey had already been ill for 24 hours. At 8:00 that evening, the family and friends went to the chapel to take communion. Kellie's parents, who were 800 miles away, were also having communion at that same time. Jerry Savelle, evangelist and friend of the family, received a word from the Lord: "As suddenly as this has come on her, it is going to go."   After donning her gown and mask, Kellie returned to Lyndsey's room and *found her talking.* Just a few minutes earlier, she had been both unconscious and delirious. It had been less than five hours since she had started taking antibiotics. From that point on, her recovery was "miraculously rapid." The next morning, the doctor was shocked to find her still alive.

Kellie states, "I guarantee you, only the blood of Jesus and the Word of God can do that." Amen and amen!

Let's examine another scenario that takes place, no doubt, tens of thousands of times each week. A church member discovers that she has cancer. She undergoes surgery and chemotherapy. The church calls a special prayer meeting and the person is prayed for, anointed with oil, and has hands laid on her by the other ladies of the church. Everyone is expectant that she will recover.

But at her semi-annual checkup, her doctor discovers that the malignancy has spread and orders more chemo. When church members hear this, some say, "I really thought God was going to heal her, but I suppose it's not His will." The patient echoes this response to her friends.

The prayers from that point on aren't as intense or as regular. When prayers are offered, they include the phrase, "If it be Thy will." Of course, we always want to be within God's perfect will. But they're no longer convinced that her healing is within His will. So the patient continues treatment, takes her prescription medication, and sees her doctor regularly to try to stop the progression of the disease—even though she feels it may not be God's will for her to be healed.

This important question arises: By continuing her treatments, is she resisting God's will? Or could it be that she is not completely convinced that it's His will *not* to heal her? And perhaps it is more convenient to blame God's will rather than our wavering faith.

The manifestations of healing may not be immediate; sometimes, it is a process. Note the wording in Mark 16:18b: "They shall lay hands on the sick, and they shall recover." *Recover* implies a process rather than an immediate result.

Do you remember Christ's first healing miracle? When Jesus came into Cana of Galilee, he met a nobleman whose son was sick in Capernaum about fifteen miles distant. He asked Jesus to come and heal his son, who was at the point of death. Jesus told him, "Except ye see signs and wonders, ye will not believe" (John 4:48). The nobleman again begged him to come before the lad died.

Jesus told him "Go thy way; thy son liveth" (v. 50). The man believed Him and started home. His servants met him on the road and happily informed him that his son was alive. He asked them when he "began to amend," and they told him it was yesterday at the seventh hour. That was exactly the time Christ had said, "Thy son liveth."

The words *began to amend* indicate that the boy didn't receive his healing instantaneously, but over a period of time, however short. So we should not be discouraged if we don't receive a miraculous, instant healing in every instance. Remember that the "gifts of healing" and the "word of knowledge" are gifts of the Holy Spirit who divides them "to every man severally as he will" (1 Corinthians 12:11b).

These gifts, which can result in miraculous healings, are not in operation continuously, but at the direction of the Holy Spirit. Therefore, we cannot dictate that they be working on our behalf at any particular time. But we can always stand on the Word of God and expect Him to hear our prayers. (For a list of healing Scriptures, see Appendix 2.)

What should we do if our healing is not manifested immediately? We should continue with any treatments our doctor(s) recommend and "take unto you the whole armor of God, that ye may be able to withstand in the evil day, and having done all, to stand" (Ephesians 6:13).

And while we're waiting in faith, we should take commonsense measures to maintain our health. We look to Christ for healing, but we have a responsibility to maintain our body in the best way we can. Even a mashed finger won't heal if it is continually hit with a hammer. We can endeavor to follow general health laws by regularly taking all medications prescribed for us by our doctors, obtaining sufficient sleep and rest, following the proper diet and by exercising if our physician will allow.

There is another frustrating situation that may confront us. We can experience a healing from the hand of the Master that far exceeds the results of medical treatment, but is less than a complete healing. What are we to do?

Several years ago, the men of our church met on Monday evenings for Bible study. In May of that year, we had finished our class and the pastor was leading the prayer of dismissal. It was quite a long prayer—and I'm glad it was. After a few moments, I felt something unusual on my eyes. It was as if someone had come up behind and cupped my eyes in their hands. A distinct warm sensation bathed my eyes. I knew it was from God.

For quite a few years, I had experienced elevated intraocular pressure as the result of glaucoma. Unfortunately, I had lost some sight due to this condition. But the next time I visited my eye doctor, he remarked, "For the first time since we placed you on eye drops, your pressure is reading normal." And it has been normal at every check-up since.

But the restoration of my vision has not yet been manifested. Why? Couldn't Christ just as easily have corrected the vision loss at the same time that He healed my eye pressure? I felt almost like the blind man in Bethsaida as recorded in Mark 8:22-25. Jesus led him out of town, spit on his eyes, and laid hands on him. When He asked him if he saw anything, he replied, "I see men as trees, walking."

He needed "a second touch." Jesus again touched his eyes and he saw clearly. If we also await another touch from the Master, we can do so in faith, believing that it will come at exactly the right time.

You will remember the time when Jesus got into a ship and went across the lake with His disciples. A violent storm came up and the boat filled with water. They awakened Jesus and He rebuked the waves. "And he said unto them, 'Where is your faith?'" (Luke 8:25).

Therefore, we should not cast away our confidence, "which hath great recompense of reward" (Hebrews 10:35).

CHAPTER 11

GAZING HEAVENWARD

The story of Christ raising Lazarus from the dead is one of the most captivating in the New Testament. In John 11, we find this account: Lazarus, who lived with sisters Mary and Martha in Bethany, had become very ill. Jesus was not close by, so the sisters sent for him, saying, "Lord, behold, he whom thou lovest is sick" (v. 3).

When Jesus received the news, He told His disciples that Lazarus' sickness would not result in death, but that it was "for the glory of God, that the Son of God might be glorified thereby" (v. 4). Jesus then waited for two more days before returning to Judea.

Jesus told His disciples that Lazarus was "sleeping," but that He was going to awaken him. They thought He meant natural sleep; He then told them plainly "Lazarus is dead" (v. 14).

When Christ and the disciples arrived in Bethany, Lazarus had already been in the grave for four days. Martha lamented that her brother would not have died if Jesus had been there (v. 21). He assured her, "Thy brother shall rise again," and asked where they had buried him. They led Him to the tomb (v. 34) and Jesus wept (v. 35).

Christ ordered them to take away the stone that covered the cave. Then He prayed and commanded Lazarus to come forth. Lazarus emerged from the grave alive and bound with grave clothes.

Did Lazarus see heaven during those four days? I've often wondered. If so, did he discuss it with Jesus and his sisters later? We're not given those answers in the Scriptures. But we do know that, even after his miraculous rising from the dead, Lazarus died again.

If Jesus tarries His coming, we know that we will all die physically. Some may die due to illness, some may die in their sleep, and others through accidents.

Uninformed persons wrongly surmise that those who believe in physical healing think they will live forever. Not true. They criticize their beliefs and sometimes make caustic remarks when they eventually die at an advanced age. "Why did they die if they believed in healing?" they ask. That's a dishonest stance. Belief in physical healing has never meant living forever.

This brings up a logical and fair question: If we become seriously ill, at age ninety for instance, should we pray and trust in God for healing, even at an advanced age?

While watching a panel discussion on this subject some years ago, I heard the following comment which I've never forgotten. One of the panelists suggested that we sincerely pray to God, asking Him if it is time for us to come to be with Him. The conclusion is simple: If He is calling us home then we will be submissive to His will. If not, we can continue to believe in faith for our physical restoration.

Serious illness can make us aware of our mortality and help us draw closer to God. If we were to die suddenly without the warning of illness, we could leave the earth with sins unforgiven and important words unsaid to our loved ones.

But God's *modus operandi* is healing. Mother Nature is actually divine healing on a lower level. What happens when you catch a virus or a cold, for example? Your white blood count rises to fight the infection. You may have a fever, and in the body's attempt to kill the germs, you sneeze and your nose runs to expel the offending invaders. If God didn't want us to remain healthy, He would not have placed these bodily defenses into service.

Moreover, Galatians 3:13 reveals that Christ redeemed us from the curse of the law through His death. But just what is the curse? The Holman Christian Standard Bible lists the following items, among others, in Deuteronomy 28: confusion, fever, inflammation, drought, blight, mildew, boils, tumors, blindness, plagues, chronic sicknesses, and "every sickness and plague not recorded in the book of this law until you are destroyed" (v. 61).

If Christ suffered and died to redeem us, then we are insulting Him by thinking that it might not be His will to provide healing for us. Let's suppose that my earthly father tells me, "Ron, I know you've had a hard time financially these past few months, so I've deposited one hundred dollars in your bank account. It's yours whenever you need it."

I need this amount to make my car payment that's due in the next five days. So I go back to him and say, "Dad, I need some money to help make my car payment. Please, please help me." It doesn't make sense, does it? Why should I beg him for something he's already provided? He would wonder about my sanity. I just need to claim and use what he has given me.

This having been said, I'm still convinced that we "see through a glass darkly" (1 Corinthians 13:12) with respect to physical healing. We don't have all the answers. There are situations where all the right prayers are offered, all the right words are spoken and still the person is not healed.

Even though we closely follow scriptural steps in our prayers, we discover we cannot manipulate God with a formula. So we sometimes observe cases of physical suffering and premature death that seem totally unfair.

We must place all our trust in Christ Who knows the beginning from the end.

My Glimpse of Heaven

What lies beyond this life for the Christian? We have all heard scattered reports of near-death experiences (NDE's) that purport to describe the things we may encounter in heaven. I'm inclined to believe some of these accounts.

Do you remember my mention of a young lady named Evelyn in Chapter 1? While in our late teens, I saw her almost daily and telephoned her every night for several months. We enjoyed movies together and conversations about family and school work. She eventually married, raised a fine family, and relocated to another state.

One afternoon, years later, I was shocked to read her obituary in the newspaper. There was no reason given for her untimely death at age forty-three. I hadn't seen or heard from her for many years and didn't inquire immediately as to the cause of her death. Her sister later informed me that she had been killed almost instantly by an automobile while walking for her health with another lady. Just a few days before the accident, she had informed friends, "My work on this earth is finished."

While she always exhibited impeccable Christian conduct in my presence, I wondered about her religious status at the time of her death. A relative assured me that she was still living a Christian life, but it didn't satisfy my curiosity completely. In the course of time, I asked the Lord to let me know about this detail. I based my request on Psalm 37:4: "Delight thyself also in the Lord; and he shall give thee the desires of thine heart." Being assured that she is with the Lord was the desire of my heart. Surely, I thought, He will let me know something and set my thoughts at ease.

I put the matter out of my mind. But about ten days later, the Lord sent me a dream—not an ordinary dream, but the kind that leaves no doubt that it's from above. I saw Evelyn in her heavenly abode, looking radiant and as young as she did when I knew her. She was sitting in a church sanctuary, wearing a navy blue dress, with a smile that reflected her overwhelming happiness there. My heart shared her joy and I turned to tell friends, "Here's Evelyn!" But when I looked back, she was gone.

The vision was so striking that it immediately verified my belief in heaven. There was no need to worry any more. She's there with the Lord she served so diligently on the earth. And she's forever free of the debilitating pain of rheumatoid arthritis from which she suffered.

I'm reminded of the last line of the hymn "Haven of Rest" that assures us "In Jesus I'm safe evermore."

APPENDIX 1: A PRAYER
FOR YOU

D ear Reader, you may use this short, model prayer to pray for your physical healing:

Dear Heavenly Father,

In the name of Your Son, Jesus Christ, the Great Physician, I come into your presence today to ask for healing for _____ (condition).

You have healed me many times before and I know that, according to Hebrews 13:8, You never change. Therefore, I believe You will once again impart Your healing power unto me.

I am standing on the following Scriptures: Isaiah 53:4-5, Psalms 103:3, 1 John 5:14-15, and Psalm 107:20.

I fully and completely believe in Your healing power and in Your mercy. Therefore, I receive healing for my condition. As of this moment, I believe I receive my healing and I expectantly look forward to the manifestation of my healing soon.

Thank You, Father for Your goodness, Your healing power, and Your mercy.

In the matchless name of your Son, the Lord Jesus Christ, I pray and believe. Amen and amen.

***

This is not a *perfect* prayer, but it expresses your needs to the Father. Come to Him expectantly. He will meet you today.

Appendix 2: Healing Scriptures

To be read **aloud** at least twice daily until your healing is manifest. Then read once daily:

But he was wounded for our transgressions; he was bruised for our iniquities: the chastisement of our peace was upon him; and with his stripes we are healed.

—Isaiah 53:5

That it might be fulfilled which was spoken by Esaias the prophet, saying, Himself took our infirmities, and bare our sicknesses.

—Matthew 8:17

Who his own self bore our sins in his own body on the tree, that we, being dead to sins, should

live unto righteousness: by whose stripes ye
were healed.

—1 Peter 2:24

Jesus Christ the same yesterday and today and
forever.

— Hebrews 13:8

Who forgiveth all thine iniquities; who healeth
all thy diseases.

— Psalm 103:3

And this is the confidence that we have in him,
that, if we ask any thing according to his will,
he heareth us. And if we know that he hear us,
whatsoever we ask, we know that we have the
petitions that we desired of him.

— 1 John 5:14-15

Beloved, I wish above all things that thou may-
est prosper and be in health, even as thy soul
prospereth.

— 3 John 2

For I will restore health unto thee, and I will heal
thee of thy wounds, saith the LORD.

— Jeremiah 30:17a

He sent his word, and healed them.

— Psalm 107:20a

My son, attend to my words; incline thine ear unto my sayings. Let them not depart from thine eyes; keep them in the midst of thine heart. For they are life unto those that find them, and health to all their flesh.

— Proverbs 4:20-22

Is any sick among you? Let him call for the elders of the church; and let them pray over him, anointing him with oil in the name of the Lord: And the prayer of faith shall save the sick, and the Lord shall raise him up; and if he hath committed sins, they shall be forgiven him. Confess your faults one to another, and pray for one another, that ye may be healed. The effectual fervent prayer of a righteous man availeth much.

— James 5:14-16

ENDNOTES

CHAPTER 1

1. J. Ronald Mikels, portions adapted from an article appearing in *SEEK the Abundant Life*, Standard Publishing, 2/21/99, p. 3. Rights reside with author.

CHAPTER 4

1. J. Ronald Mikels, adapted from an article appearing in *FGBMFI VOICE*, November, 1977, p. 8. Used by permission.

CHAPTER 5

1. Charles Capps, *Hope, A Partner to Faith,* Harrison House, P. O. Box 35035, Tulsa, OK 74153, © 1986, pp. 17-21.

CHAPTER 6

1. Catherine Marshall, *A Man Called Peter,* Crest Books, © 1951, pp. 173-181.
2. Keith Moore, *Key to Greater Grace,* vol. 3 of video series, Moore Life Ministries, P. O. Box 1010, Branson, MO 65615, © 2002.

CHAPTER 7

1. *Dictionary of Pentecostal and Charismatic Movements,* Regency Reference Library, Zondervan Publishers, © 1988, p. 758.
2. Kenneth E. Hagin, *The Name of Jesus,* Legacy Edition, Rhema Bible Church, P. O. Box 50126, Tulsa, OK 74150, © 2006, pp. 133-134.
3. J. Ronald Mikels, *VISTA,* Wesleyan Publishing House, June, 1990, p. 8. Rights reside with author.
4. *Answered Prayers,* a *Guideposts* book, Carmel, NY, © 2000 p. 54-55.

CHAPTER 8

1. Kenneth E. Hagin, "Calling Those Things That Be Not," Healing Classics Tape Series, Kenneth E. Hagin Ministries, P. O. Box 50126, Tulsa, OK 74150, © 1975.

CHAPTER 10

1. Kellie Copeland, *Protecting Your Family in Dangerous Times*, (Tulsa: Harrison House Publishers, copyright 2002) pp. 110-119.